THE BAT BUSINESS REVOLUTION

How to Create a Thriving Enterprise That Benefits both You and the Environment

Jeanelle K. Douglas

Table of Contents

Introduction

Starting a bat colony is a rewarding venture that not only offers a fascinating glimpse into the natural world but also contributes significantly to the health and balance of local ecosystems. Bats, often misunderstood and undervalued, are crucial for the environment. They play vital roles in pollinating plants, dispersing seeds, and controlling insect populations, which can otherwise devastate crops and spread diseases. Despite their importance, bats face numerous threats, including habitat loss, climate change, and diseases like white-nose syndrome. By establishing a bat colony, individuals and communities can take an active role in conserving these essential creatures and fostering biodiversity in their local areas.

The journey to creating a thriving bat colony begins with understanding these unique mammals—their habits, preferences, and the types of environments they thrive in. It's essential to debunk common myths that paint bats in a negative light and to appreciate the diversity and ecological importance of these nocturnal creatures. Legal and safety considerations are paramount to ensure that the initiative complies with local wildlife protection laws and safeguards both the bats and the human participants involved.

Creating suitable habitats, such as bat houses, requires careful planning and consideration of design, location, and the specific needs of bat species in the region. Successfully attracting bats to these new homes involves creating an inviting environment, complete with adequate food sources and water. Moreover, maintaining and monitoring the colony provides valuable insights into bat behavior and population health, contributing to broader conservation efforts.

Engaging the community is a critical component of this endeavor. By sharing knowledge and fostering an appreciation for bats, individuals can dispel myths and encourage broader support for bat conservation. Collaborating with local wildlife organizations and participating in citizen science projects can amplify the impact of these efforts.

This guide is designed to navigate the intricate process of starting and sustaining a bat colony. Through detailed explanations, practical advice, and a focus on conservation, it aims to empower individuals to contribute positively to their local ecosystems and the global environment by providing safe havens for one of nature's most remarkable and beneficial animals.

Importance of Bats in Ecosystems

Bats, with their nocturnal flights and distinctive silhouettes against the twilight sky, play an indispensable role in the health and vitality of ecosystems around the globe. These creatures, often shrouded in mystery and misconceptions, are fundamental to the balance of nature, performing several critical ecological functions that benefit both the environment and human populations.

One of the most significant roles of bats is their contribution to pollination. As they flit from flower to flower in search of nectar, bats inadvertently transfer pollen, facilitating the reproduction of many plants. This pollination is crucial for the production of fruits that form the diet of countless other species, including humans. In regions like the tropics and the desert, where bats are the primary or exclusive pollinators for certain plants, their role is even more critical. Plants such as agave and the iconic saguaro cactus rely on bats for their survival, which in turn supports industries and local economies, such as tequila production in Mexico.

Beyond pollination, bats are also key players in seed dispersal. Fruit-eating bats spread seeds far and wide, helping to regenerate forests and maintain diverse plant communities. This dispersal is essential for the health of tropical forests and the species that inhabit them, ensuring forests remain resilient and can recover from disturbances such as deforestation or natural disasters.

Perhaps the most widely recognized benefit of bats is their unparalleled ability to control insect populations. By consuming vast quantities of insects nightly, bats act as natural pest control, protecting crops from damage and reducing the need for chemical pesticides. This service is invaluable for agriculture, saving farmers billions of dollars annually in pest management costs. Moreover, by controlling insect populations, bats also help to reduce the spread of insect-borne diseases to humans.

Bats contribute to the nutrient cycle within ecosystems. The guano (bat droppings) produced by bat colonies is a highly effective fertilizer, rich in nutrients that promote plant growth. This guano can rejuvenate depleted soils and is sought after for use in gardening and agriculture.

Despite these critical roles, bat populations face significant threats from habitat destruction, climate change, and diseases such as white-nose syndrome. The decline of bat populations can have far-reaching consequences for ecosystems and human economies alike, highlighting the importance of conservation efforts to protect these vital creatures.

In essence, bats are unsung heroes of the natural world, providing services that sustain the health of ecosystems and support agricultural and economic activities. Their preservation is not just a matter of ecological responsibility but also one of ensuring the continued wellbeing of human societies that benefit immensely from the myriad ecological services bats provide.

Benefits of Starting a Bat Colony

Starting a bat colony offers a myriad of benefits, both to the natural world and to human communities. Bats, often misunderstood and undervalued, play a critical role in maintaining healthy ecosystems. By providing a habitat for these nocturnal creatures, we support their survival and contribute to the balance of nature in several impactful ways.

Bats are renowned for their pest control abilities. A single bat can consume thousands of insects each night, including mosquitoes and pests that damage agricultural crops. This natural pest control is not only beneficial for the environment but also provides economic advantages by reducing the need for chemical pesticides, which can have harmful side effects on the health of ecosystems and human populations alike.

Moreover, bats are vital pollinators and seed dispersers for many plants. In regions where bats are active pollinators, they contribute to the reproduction of fruits and plants, including some that are crucial to human diets and economies, such as bananas, avocados, and agave. By starting a bat colony, we help ensure the continuation of these essential natural processes, supporting local agriculture and biodiversity.

Creating a bat colony also has conservation benefits. Many bat species are under threat due to habitat loss, climate change, and diseases such as white-nose syndrome. Providing safe roosting sites can help stabilize and increase local bat populations, contributing to the overall health of bat species and the ecosystems they inhabit.

Additionally, bat colonies can serve as educational tools. They offer unique opportunities for learning and engagement with nature, allowing communities, schools, and individuals to observe bat behavior firsthand, learn about their role in the environment, and understand the importance of conservation efforts. This can foster a greater appreciation for wildlife and encourage a more environmentally conscious mindset among participants.

Bat colonies can enhance community involvement and environmental stewardship. By engaging in bat conservation, communities can come together to work on a shared project that has positive implications for the environment and local biodiversity.

This can strengthen community bonds, promote outdoor activities, and inspire other conservation initiatives.

Understanding Bats

Understanding bats is crucial for appreciating their role in ecosystems and the importance of conserving their populations. Bats, belonging to the order Chiroptera, are the only mammals capable of sustained flight, which allows them to play unique roles in the natural world. Their diversity, with over 1,400 species worldwide, makes them incredibly versatile and essential for the health of various environments.

Bats are often categorized into two main groups:

Microbats and megabats. Microbats are typically smaller, use echolocation to navigate and find their prey, and are found in a wide range of habitats across the globe. They are known for their insectivorous diets, although some species also feed on fruit, nectar, or even small vertebrates and blood. Megabats, or fruit bats, tend to be larger, rely on their keen sense of sight and smell rather than echolocation, and are primarily found in tropical and subtropical regions. These bats usually have a diet consisting of fruit, nectar, and pollen, playing crucial roles in pollination and seed dispersal.

The behavior and lifecycle of bats are as varied as their diets. Most bats are nocturnal, active at night when they hunt for food, using their acute echolocation abilities or senses to navigate in the dark. Their roosting habits vary widely; some species prefer the secluded safety of caves, while others may roost in trees, under bridges, or in buildings. Bats typically have slow reproductive rates, with most species giving birth to only one pup per year. This slow reproduction makes their populations particularly vulnerable to threats.

Bats play vital ecological roles. As mentioned, insectivorous bats help control pest populations, significantly benefiting agriculture and reducing the need for chemical pesticides. Fruit and nectar-feeding bats are critical pollinators and seed dispersers for many plants, some of which are commercially important to humans. Their activities support forest regeneration and diversity.

Despite their ecological importance, bats face numerous threats, including habitat destruction, climate change, pesticides, and diseases such as white-nose syndrome, which has decimated certain bat populations in North America. Public perception of bats is often negative, rooted in myths and misunderstandings, which can hinder conservation efforts.

Understanding bats involves dispelling these myths and recognizing their significance to ecosystems and human economies. It also entails learning about their behaviors, habitats, and the challenges they face. By gaining a deeper appreciation for bats, we can better support their conservation and the critical roles they play in maintaining the health of our planet.

Species of Bats Suitable for Colonies

The species of bats suitable for colonies in a given area depend largely on the region's climate, available habitats, and the specific needs of different bat species. Not all bats are equally suited to live in close proximity to humans or in bat houses, so it's important to focus on species that are known to adapt well to such conditions. Here are examples of bat species that have shown adaptability to living in colonies near human dwellings and are often targeted for conservation efforts through the creation of bat houses or the enhancement of natural roost sites.

In North America:

Little Brown Bat (Myotis lucifugus): This species is widespread across North America and is one of the most common species to take up residence in bat houses. They are known for their insect-eating habits, consuming a significant number of mosquitos and other pests.

Big Brown Bat (Eptesicus fuscus): Another common species in North America, big brown bats are adaptable and often roost in buildings and bat houses. They play a critical role in controlling pest populations.

Mexican Free-tailed Bat (Tadarida brasiliensis): Renowned for their large, dense colonies, especially in the southern U.S. and Mexico, these bats are excellent at controlling agricultural pests.

In Europe:

- **Common Pipistrelle (Pipistrellus pipistrellus):** One of the smallest and most common bat species in Europe, the common pipistrelle is often found in gardens and near human habitation, making it suitable for bat house projects.

- **Soprano Pipistrelle (Pipistrellus pygmaeus):** Similar to the common pipistrelle, this species also readily takes to bat houses and plays a significant role in insect control.

In Australia:

- **Gould's Wattled Bat (Chalinolobus gouldii):** Found across Australia, these bats are adaptable to a variety of habitats and can benefit from bat house installations.

- **Chocolate Wattled Bat (Chalinolobus morio):** Another species that is known to use bat boxes, providing important insect control services.

In Tropical Regions:

- Lesser Short-nosed Fruit Bat (Cynopterus brachyotis): In regions where fruit bats are prevalent, this species is known to adapt to human-modified habitats and can help pollinate plants and disperse seeds.

When considering starting a bat colony, it's crucial to research which species are native to your area and their specific habitat requirements. Conservation efforts should aim to support native species, enhancing biodiversity and ecosystem health. Encouraging the right species involves creating the proper environment for them, including the correct type of bat houses, the ideal placement, and ensuring there are suitable food sources and water nearby. Collaboration with local wildlife experts or bat conservation groups can provide valuable guidance in selecting the appropriate species and implementing effective conservation strategies.

Bat Behavior and Lifecycle

Bats exhibit a fascinating array of behaviors and life cycles that vary widely among the different species. Despite this diversity, there are commonalities in their behaviors and life stages that underscore their ecological importance and the challenges they face.

At the heart of bat behavior is their nocturnal activity. Bats are primarily active at night, when they leave their roosts to feed. This behavior is closely tied to their use of echolocation, a sophisticated biological sonar system. Echolocation allows bats to navigate and hunt for food in complete darkness, emitting ultrasonic sounds that bounce off objects and return as echoes. The bats interpret these echoes to determine the location, size, and even the type of prey or obstacles in their path. This remarkable ability showcases bats' adaptation to their ecological niche, allowing them to be effective hunters of night-flying insects and, for some species, key pollinators of night-blooming plants.

The lifecycle of a bat begins with mating, which can occur at various times of the year depending on the species. Some species mate in the fall, with females storing sperm through winter hibernation and fertilizing their eggs in the spring. Others mate in spring or during their active summer months. Pregnancy and gestation periods vary among species but are generally lengthy compared to other mammals of similar size, lasting anywhere from 40 days to six months. This extended gestation is due in part to the bats' slow metabolism during periods of inactivity or hibernation.

Most bats give birth to a single pup per year, a reproductive strategy that emphasizes the survival of each offspring. At birth, bat pups are exceptionally vulnerable, often born without fur and with their eyes closed. They are, however, remarkably developed in other ways, capable of clinging to their mothers with strong feet and even capable of vocalizations. Maternal care is crucial during this stage; mothers nurse their pups with milk, and in some species, they may carry their young during feeding flights if the roost is not secure.

As the pups grow, they learn to fly and hunt, a process that can take several weeks to months depending on the species. This period is critical for their survival, as young bats must quickly hone their echolocation skills and flying ability to evade predators and successfully forage for food. By the end of the summer or the active season, these young bats must be fully independent, as they will face the challenges of migration or hibernation.

Hibernation is another key aspect of bat behavior, particularly for species living in temperate regions where food becomes scarce in winter. Bats enter a state of torpor, significantly reducing their metabolic rate to conserve energy. They seek out hibernacula—sites like caves or mines with stable, cool temperatures ideal for hibernation. During this time, bats can survive on their fat reserves, but they remain vulnerable to disturbances and environmental changes that can deplete their energy reserves prematurely.

Migration is observed in some bat species, which travel to warmer climates or more abundant feeding grounds in response to seasonal changes. These migrations can span hundreds to thousands of miles and are critical for the survival of these species, ensuring access to food and suitable roosting sites throughout the year.

The lifecycle of bats, marked by periods of intense activity and long bouts of rest, reflects their adaptation to diverse and often challenging environments. Understanding these behaviors and life stages is crucial for conserving bat populations, as it informs strategies to protect their habitats, support their reproductive success, and ensure the continuation of their vital roles in ecosystems around the world.

Common Misconceptions about Bats

Bats have long been enveloped in mystery and misconceptions, many of which stem from myths, folklore, and their nocturnal nature. These misconceptions often paint bats in a negative light, overshadowing their crucial role in ecosystems around the world.

Understanding and dispelling these myths is essential for bat conservation and for fostering a more positive perception of these remarkable creatures.

One common misconception is that all bats carry rabies. While bats, like many mammals, can contract rabies, the incidence of rabies in bat populations is extremely low. Most bats do not have rabies; however, because rabid bats are more likely to be found on the ground and come into contact with humans, it may seem as though a higher percentage of the population is infected. It's essential to avoid handling bats but also to recognize that their role in ecosystems far outweighs the small risk they pose.

Another widespread myth is that bats are blind. This couldn't be further from the truth; bats have eyesight that ranges from good to excellent, depending on the species. While it's true that many species rely on echolocation to navigate and find their prey in the dark, this doesn't mean they are blind. Echolocation is an advanced, sophisticated means of sensory perception that allows bats to "see" their environment in complete darkness by emitting sounds and listening for the echoes returned by objects in their path.

Bats are also often thought to be pests. However, bats are incredibly beneficial to humans and the environment. Insectivorous bats consume millions of insects each night, including pests that damage agricultural crops and spread disease, such as mosquitoes. Fruit and nectar-eating bats play critical roles in pollination and seed dispersal, supporting the growth of many plants that humans rely on for food, medicine, and timber.

The idea that bats frequently attack humans is another myth. Bats are generally shy and avoid contact with humans. Most species are more interested in pursuing their natural prey than interacting with people. When bats are seen flying close to humans, they are usually feeding on insects attracted to human activity, not seeking out humans themselves.

The association of bats with haunted houses and dark, scary places has contributed to a negative image that belies their ecological importance. Bats often roost in caves, abandoned buildings, and other secluded places simply because these habitats offer the conditions they need for roosting, not because they prefer spooky locations. In reality, bats are fascinating animals that play critical roles in maintaining healthy environments.

By dispelling these common misconceptions about bats, we can foster a more accurate and appreciative understanding of their place in the natural world and the importance of conserving their populations for the health of global ecosystems.

Legal and Safety Considerations

When embarking on the journey to start a bat colony, it's imperative to navigate the landscape of legal and safety considerations to ensure the project is both lawful and safe for humans and bats alike. These considerations are foundational to creating a sustainable environment where bats can thrive without causing unintended harm to the community or the bats themselves.

Legal considerations vary significantly depending on geographic location. Many countries and regions have specific wildlife protection laws that regulate interactions with bats, including their relocation, the modification of their habitats, and the installation of bat houses. Some bat species are protected under national or international conservation laws due to their declining populations and the critical roles they play in ecosystems. Before starting a bat colony, it's essential to research and comply with local wildlife protection statutes, which may require permits or guidance from wildlife authorities. Engaging with these authorities not only ensures legal compliance but also provides access to expert advice on how to successfully and responsibly encourage bat populations.

Safety considerations are twofold, concerning both human and bat welfare. Bats, like any wild animals, can carry diseases, including rabies. While the risk of transmission to humans is low, it's crucial to never handle bats with bare hands. In the event of finding a sick or injured bat, contact local wildlife rehabilitation professionals who are equipped and trained to care for them safely. Installing bat houses away from direct human interaction zones, like play areas or main entrances, can minimize direct contact between bats and humans, reducing any associated risks.

For the bats' safety, proper installation and maintenance of bat houses are key. Bat houses should be placed in areas that protect bats from predators and provide optimal temperature and humidity levels for the species you aim to attract. This involves careful consideration of height, orientation, and proximity to water sources and feeding areas. Regular maintenance checks are necessary to ensure the structures remain safe and habitable over time, taking care not to disturb the occupants.

Another aspect of safety is the ecological impact of introducing a bat colony to a new area. It's important to ensure that the project supports native species and does not disrupt local ecosystems. Introducing non-native species or excessively concentrating bats in one area can lead to ecological imbalances, affecting other wildlife and plant populations.

Public education and awareness are critical components of the legal and safety considerations surrounding bat conservation projects. Informing the community about the benefits of bats, the purpose of the bat colony, and how to coexist safely with these nocturnal neighbors can alleviate fears and misconceptions. It also fosters a sense of stewardship and appreciation for the natural world.

Regulations and Permissions

Navigating regulations and securing permissions is a critical step in establishing a bat colony, as these legal frameworks are designed to protect both the bats and the community. The specifics of these regulations can vary widely depending on the location, as different countries, states, and even municipalities may have their own rules concerning wildlife conservation and habitat modification.

It's important to identify whether the bat species you intend to support are protected under any local, regional, or international conservation laws. Many bat species are classified as threatened or endangered due to factors like habitat loss, pesticide use, and diseases such as white-nose syndrome. As a result, activities that could impact these species, including habitat creation or alteration, may require specific permissions or permits from wildlife authorities.

To navigate these legal waters, start by contacting your local wildlife conservation office or environmental protection agency. These bodies can provide guidance on the necessary steps to legally establish a bat colony. They can inform you about the specific permits required, the application process, and any guidelines you must follow to ensure your project does not negatively impact the bat populations or their habitats.

In addition to securing permissions related to bat conservation, you may also need to consider zoning laws or regulations related to land use, especially if you plan to install bat houses or modify landscapes on your property. Certain areas may have restrictions on the types of structures that can be erected or specific requirements regarding their placement. For example, bat houses must be placed at a certain height and in locations that provide safe and easy access for bats, which may not align with local building codes or homeowners' association rules.

Engaging with the community and local authorities early in the planning process can help preempt any legal or regulatory hurdles. Public hearings or community meetings might be necessary if your project has the potential to impact shared resources or community spaces. Gaining community support can be crucial, as it not only facilitates smoother project implementation but also promotes a broader understanding and appreciation of bat conservation efforts.

Moreover, collaborating with local environmental groups, bat conservation organizations, or universities can provide additional resources and credibility to your project. These partnerships may offer expert advice, assist with the permit application process, and help navigate the complexities of local wildlife regulations. They can also provide valuable data about local bat populations, their habitats, and conservation needs, ensuring that your project contributes positively to the local ecosystem.

Health and Safety Guidelines

When initiating a project to establish a bat colony, adhering to health and safety guidelines is paramount to protect both the bats and the human community involved. These guidelines are designed to mitigate risks, ensuring a safe environment for everyone. Understanding and implementing these measures can prevent potential health issues and ensure the project's success in a safe and responsible manner.

One of the primary health concerns associated with bats is the risk of disease transmission, notably rabies. While the percentage of bats infected with rabies is low, it's crucial to minimize contact between bats and humans. Individuals should never handle bats with bare hands. If there's a need to assist an injured or grounded bat, it's important to wear thick gloves and preferably contact local wildlife rehabilitation professionals who are equipped and trained to handle bats safely.

Educating the community about bats and disease transmission is essential. Providing clear information about the low risk of rabies transmission, while also emphasizing the importance of not touching or handling bats, can alleviate fears and misunderstandings. For projects involving the installation of bat houses, ensure they are placed in areas that are not frequently accessed by people, especially children and pets, to reduce the likelihood of direct contact.

Another aspect of health and safety involves the proper design and maintenance of bat houses. Bat houses should be constructed and installed following guidelines that ensure they are safe, durable, and suitable for bat habitation. This includes using non-toxic materials, ensuring stability and security from predators, and placing the houses at an appropriate height to prevent accidents or disturbances.

Monitoring the bat colony also requires safety precautions. Those involved in maintenance or observational activities should be aware of the proper times and methods to approach bat houses to minimize disturbance to the bats and reduce the risk of exposure to any pathogens. It's also vital to respect the bats' hibernation and maternity seasons, avoiding any intrusive activities during these sensitive periods.

In regions where bat guano (droppings) accumulates near human habitation, there's a potential risk of respiratory issues from inhaling dust that contains fungal spores, such as those of Histoplasma capsulatum, which can cause histoplasmosis. Guidelines for safely cleaning areas affected by guano should be followed, including wearing protective gear such as gloves, masks, and goggles to prevent inhalation and direct contact with the guano.

Engagement with health and wildlife professionals throughout the project can provide additional insights and guidance on managing health and safety risks. Collaboration with local health departments, wildlife agencies, and bat conservation groups can offer support and resources, ensuring that your efforts to promote bat conservation adhere to the best practices in health and safety.

Planning Your Bat Colony

Planning your bat colony is a thoughtful process that requires consideration of various factors to ensure the success and sustainability of the project. It begins with a deep understanding of bats and their needs, as well as an awareness of the local environment and community. The goal is to create a welcoming habitat for bats that also coexists harmoniously with human neighbors.

The first step in planning is choosing a suitable location for your bat colony. This involves identifying areas that are not only attractive to bats but also considerate of human activities and concerns. Bats prefer locations that are close to water sources, as water attracts insects, which are a primary food source for many bat species. Additionally, the chosen site should offer protection from predators and extreme weather conditions, with adequate exposure to sunlight to keep the bats warm.

Assessing habitat requirements is another crucial aspect of planning. Different bat species have varying needs in terms of roosting spaces and environmental conditions. Some species may prefer open spaces for their roosts, while others might seek more enclosed areas. Understanding the specific requirements of the species you aim to attract is essential for creating a suitable habitat. This may involve constructing bat houses that mimic natural roosting sites, providing access to water, and ensuring there is an abundance of food sources nearby.

Timing is also a key factor in planning your bat colony. Most bat species in temperate regions are most active during the warmer months and hibernate or migrate during the winter. Therefore, the installation of bat houses or the enhancement of natural habitats should ideally be completed before the bats return from migration or emerge from hibernation. This gives the bats time to discover and adapt to the new roosting sites before they are needed for the breeding season.

Engaging with the community and local authorities early in the planning process can help address any concerns and foster support for the project. This includes ensuring that all necessary permissions and regulations are followed, as well as educating the public about the benefits of bats and how the project will be managed safely and responsibly.

Planning your bat colony is an ongoing process that doesn't end once the bats have been attracted to the site. Regular monitoring and maintenance of the habitat are essential to ensure it remains suitable and safe for the bats over time. This may involve cleaning and repairing bat houses, managing vegetation, and continuing to engage with the community to share the successes of the project and the positive impact of the bats on the local ecosystem.

Planning a bat colony is a comprehensive process that requires careful consideration of the needs of both the bats and the human community. By choosing a suitable location, assessing habitat requirements, considering the timing, engaging with the community, and committing to ongoing maintenance, you can create a successful bat colony that benefits both local ecosystems and the people who live within them.

Choosing a Suitable Location

Choosing a suitable location for your bat colony is fundamental to its success and the well-being of the bats. The ideal location strikes a balance between the natural requirements of the bats and the proximity to human habitats, ensuring a harmonious coexistence. Several key factors must be considered to select a location that encourages bats to roost and thrive.

Proximity to Water Sources: Bats require access to water for drinking and foraging. Water bodies attract insects, which are a primary food source for many bat species. Locations near rivers, lakes, streams, or even artificial water bodies like ponds can significantly increase the attractiveness of the site for bats. The closer the water source, the higher the likelihood of bats choosing to roost nearby.

Food Availability: A rich supply of insects is crucial for insectivorous bats. Therefore, areas with abundant vegetation that attract insects, such as gardens, parks, or natural forests, are ideal. Avoiding the use of pesticides in these areas is also important to ensure a healthy food supply for the bats.

Sun Exposure: Bat houses need to be warm, especially for mother bats raising pups. The location should therefore offer good sun exposure. In temperate climates, south-facing orientations are often recommended to maximize sunlight exposure. However, the required sun exposure can vary based on regional climate, so local guidelines should be consulted to determine the best orientation.

Protection from Predators: Safety from predators is crucial. Locations that are too accessible to predators like cats or raccoons may deter bats. Bat houses should be placed high enough, typically 12 to 20 feet above the ground, to reduce the risk from ground predators. Avoiding locations too close to tree branches or other structures that predators can use for access is also advisable.

Avoidance of High Traffic Areas: While it's beneficial to have the bat colony close enough to human areas to promote ecological benefits, placing bat houses directly over busy paths or right next to living spaces can lead to potential conflicts. Choose locations that are somewhat removed from high traffic areas to minimize disturbances to both bats and humans.

Natural Wind Shelter: Locations that provide some shelter from high winds create a more stable and comfortable environment for bats. However, adequate ventilation is necessary to prevent the bat house from becoming too stuffy and hot. Strategic placement can utilize natural landscapes for shelter while still ensuring proper air circulation.

Altitude and Open Space: Bats prefer locations that allow easy access to their roosting spots. Sites with open spaces free of obstructions can facilitate bats' entry and exit from their roosts. The altitude at which a bat house is mounted can also impact its attractiveness, with higher placements often being more appealing to bats.

In essence, choosing a suitable location for a bat colony involves a careful evaluation of the natural environment and its compatibility with bat biology. By considering these key factors, you can create a habitat that supports the health and proliferation of bats, contributing positively to the local ecosystem and biodiversity. Collaboration with local wildlife experts and bat conservation organizations can provide additional insights and guidance in selecting the perfect spot for your bat colony.

Assessing Habitat Requirements

Assessing habitat requirements is a pivotal step in planning a successful bat colony, as it involves understanding the specific needs of bats in order to create an environment where they can thrive. This process entails a detailed examination of the natural behaviors, preferences, and lifecycle of bats, alongside an evaluation of the local ecosystem to ensure it can support these needs.

Bats have a diverse range of habitat requirements, influenced by their species-specific behaviors, feeding habits, and roosting preferences. The primary habitat components to consider include roosting sites, foraging areas, water sources, and landscape features that facilitate their nightly activities.

Roosting Sites: Bats need safe places to roost during the day and rear their young. This can include natural features like caves, tree cavities, and rock crevices, or man-made structures such as bat houses. The design of bat houses should mimic natural roosting conditions as closely as possible, providing adequate space, temperature control, and protection from predators. The size, shape, and internal structure of the bat house can significantly impact its suitability for different bat species.

Foraging Areas: The availability of feeding grounds close to roosting sites is critical. Bats are insectivores, pollinators, or fruit eaters, depending on the species, so the habitat must offer a plentiful and consistent supply of food. This is typically achieved through the presence of water bodies and varied vegetation, which attract insects and support the growth of plants that produce fruits or flowers.

Water Sources: Access to fresh water for drinking is essential for bats. Proximity to streams, ponds, or lakes not only supports the bats' hydration needs but also enhances the area's suitability as a foraging ground, as water bodies attract a variety of insects.

Landscape Features: The physical characteristics of the landscape play a significant role in bat navigation and foraging efficiency. Open spaces allow for easier flight and insect hunting, while connectivity between different landscape elements (such as patches of forest or meadow) supports bats in navigating between roosting and feeding areas. Features that disrupt this connectivity, like busy roads or large, open areas without cover, can hinder bats' movements and reduce the habitat's overall suitability.

In addition to these physical requirements, assessing habitat suitability also involves considering factors like climate and human activity. The climate influences the types of vegetation available for foraging and the suitability of roosting conditions, while human activities can impact bats through noise, light pollution, and habitat fragmentation.

Conducting a thorough assessment of habitat requirements involves both research and on-the-ground evaluation. Engaging with local wildlife experts, conservation organizations, and academic institutions can provide valuable insights into the specific needs of bat species in your area. These partnerships can also offer guidance on how to enhance the habitat for bats, whether through planting native vegetation, installing bat houses, or protecting existing natural features.

Ultimately, assessing habitat requirements is about creating a comprehensive support system for bats, one that mirrors their natural environments as closely as possible. By carefully considering the needs of bats and the characteristics of the local ecosystem, it's possible to develop a habitat that encourages bats to establish a colony, thereby contributing to the health of the local ecosystem and biodiversity.

Timing When to Start Your Colony

The timing of when to start your bat colony is crucial for its success and can significantly influence the likelihood of bats taking up residence in the habitats you provide. This timing revolves around the bats' natural life cycles, including migration patterns, breeding seasons, and hibernation periods, which vary depending on the species and the geographical location.

Migration and Seasonal Activity

Many bat species in temperate regions migrate between summer roosts and winter hibernacula. These migrations are closely tied to the seasons and the availability of food. In spring, bats return from their winter hibernation sites and begin looking for suitable places to roost during the warmer months. This period, often from mid-March to late May, depending on your local climate, is ideal for installing bat houses or enhancing natural habitats. By setting up before the bats return or shortly after, you give them the opportunity to discover and adopt the new roosting sites for the summer.

Breeding Season

The breeding season is another critical time to consider. Bats typically have their young in late spring to early summer. The maternity season, when female bats gather to give birth and rear their young, requires stable, warm environments. Installing bat houses well before this period ensures they are available when needed. It's also advisable to avoid disturbing bat colonies during the maternity season, as interference could lead to the abandonment of the roost by the mother bats, putting the pups at risk.

Hibernation Considerations

For regions with cold winters, bats will seek out hibernation sites in late fall, where they will remain until the weather warms up again in spring. While some bat species hibernate in caves and mines, others may use tree cavities or even bat houses if the conditions are right. Enhancements to winter habitats should be completed by early fall or postponed until spring to avoid disturbing hibernating bats.

Year-round Residents

In tropical and subtropical regions, where temperatures remain relatively stable throughout the year, bats may not migrate or hibernate. In these areas, habitat enhancements can be made at almost any time, though it's still beneficial to avoid major disturbances during the breeding season.

Ongoing Maintenance

After the initial establishment of the bat colony, ongoing maintenance of the habitat is essential. This should be planned during times when it's least likely to disturb the bats. Late winter to early spring, before bats return from migration or come out of hibernation, is usually the best time for maintenance work on bat houses and other roosting structures.

The best time to start your bat colony is when it aligns with the natural behaviors and needs of the bat species you aim to attract. This ensures that the habitats are ready and available when bats are seeking new roosts or preparing for the breeding season. Proper timing, combined with an understanding of bat life cycles and seasonal activities, can greatly increase the chances of bats adopting the habitats you provide and the overall success of your bat conservation efforts.

Creating Bat Habitats

Creating bat habitats is a rewarding endeavor that involves careful planning and consideration to ensure that the spaces you create are both welcoming and suitable for bat populations. The essence of creating bat habitats lies in understanding the needs of bats and replicating, as closely as possible, the natural environments they prefer for roosting, breeding, and hibernating. This effort often focuses on two main strategies: designing and building bat houses and enhancing natural habitats to encourage bats to roost in specific areas.

Designing and building bat houses is a popular and effective way to support bat populations. These structures provide bats with safe places to roost, away from predators and the elements. Bat houses should mimic the crevices and cavities that bats use in their natural environments. They need to be narrow and dark, with rough internal surfaces for bats to cling to. The dimensions and design can vary based on the species you aim to attract, but all bat houses should have adequate ventilation to prevent overheating and enough depth to protect bats from predators. Using untreated, sustainably sourced wood and non-toxic paints or stains is crucial to ensure the health and safety of the bat colony. Placement is also key; bat houses should be mounted on poles or buildings, facing south or southeast in most climates to ensure they receive sufficient sunlight to maintain a warm temperature inside, but this can vary based on local conditions.

In building bat houses, enhancing natural habitats is essential for creating comprehensive bat-friendly environments. This involves preserving or restoring natural features that bats use for roosting, such as dead trees, caves, and abandoned buildings. It also means ensuring a healthy ecosystem with plenty of water and food sources. Planting night-scented flowers, native vegetation, and maintaining water bodies can attract insects, providing food for bats and making the habitat more appealing. Reducing or eliminating pesticide use in these areas is critical to ensure bats have access to safe, nutritious food sources.

Water features are particularly important in bat habitats. Bats need water for drinking and as a source of insects. Creating or maintaining ponds, streams, or even artificial water features can significantly enhance the habitat's attractiveness to bats. These water sources should be designed with bat safety in mind, incorporating shallow edges or sloped sides to prevent bats from drowning.

The overarching goal in creating bat habitats is to provide safe, comfortable environments for bats to live and reproduce. This requires an ongoing commitment to habitat maintenance and monitoring, ensuring that the structures remain in good condition and the natural features continue to provide the resources bats need.

Engaging with local conservation groups and utilizing resources from bat conservation organizations can provide valuable guidance and support in this process.

Creating bat habitats is about more than just building structures or planting gardens; it's about fostering ecosystems where bats can thrive. This not only benefits the bats but also enhances local biodiversity and contributes to the health of the environment, making it a deeply fulfilling project for anyone concerned with wildlife conservation and ecological stewardship.

Designing and Building Bat Houses

Designing and building bat houses is a detailed process that requires attention to specific requirements to ensure these artificial roosts are attractive and suitable for bats. Bat houses serve as safe havens for bats, offering them shelter from predators and harsh weather conditions while supporting local ecosystems through pest control and pollination. The key to a successful bat house lies in its design, location, and installation.

Design Considerations

The internal design of a bat house should mimic the tight, dark crevices that bats favor in their natural roosting environments. This means creating narrow chambers, typically between ¾ inch to 1 inch wide, allowing bats to cluster closely for warmth and safety. The inside surface of these chambers should be roughened or grooved, or equipped with mesh, to provide bats with a surface they can easily cling to. This can be achieved by scoring the wood with saw cuts or applying a non-toxic, water-based paint mixed with sand or grit.

The exterior design should focus on durability and climate regulation. Using materials that withstand weathering, like untreated, exterior-grade plywood or cedar, ensures the longevity of the bat house. The color of the bat house is crucial for temperature control and will vary based on geographic location. In cooler climates, darker colors are preferred to absorb more heat, while in warmer areas, lighter colors help keep the bat house cool.

Size and Capacity

The size of the bat house can influence its attractiveness to bats. Larger bat houses tend to have higher occupancy rates, as they provide more stable internal temperatures. Multi-chambered bat houses offer more space and varying microclimates within the same structure, accommodating more bats and increasing the chances of colonization.

Location and Orientation

Location is paramount in bat house success. Bat houses should be placed in areas that receive six to eight hours of direct sunlight daily, ideally facing south or southeast to catch the morning sun. They should be mounted at least 12 to 20 feet above ground, away from predatory threats and with clear flight paths for easy bat access. Proximity to water sources and foraging areas significantly enhances the attractiveness of the bat house.

Installation Tips

When installing bat houses, stability against wind and weather is important. Mounting them on poles or the sides of buildings can offer better temperature stability compared to trees, which can be too shady and accessible to predators. Ensure the bat house is securely attached to prevent swaying, which could deter bats from roosting.

Maintenance and Monitoring

After installation, periodic checks are recommended to assess occupancy and condition. Maintenance may involve repairing or repainting the bat house to preserve its structure and appeal. Monitoring can also provide valuable data on bat preferences and behavior, contributing to broader conservation efforts.

Adhering to these design and building principles, you can create a welcoming and suitable environment for bats. Not only does this support bat conservation, but it also benefits local agriculture and communities by encouraging natural pest control and pollination. Engaging in the design and construction of bat houses is a tangible way to contribute to environmental stewardship and biodiversity.

Materials and Tools Needed

Creating a bat house is a project that requires specific materials and tools to ensure the finished product is safe, durable, and attractive to bats. Using the right materials and tools will greatly increase your chances of successfully attracting bats to your new habitat. Here's a comprehensive list of materials and tools typically needed for building a bat house:

Materials

1. Wood: Exterior-grade plywood (at least 1/2 inch thick) or cedar boards are recommended for their durability and resistance to weathering. Avoid pressure-treated wood due to chemicals that can be harmful to bats.

2. Roughening Material: Non-toxic water-based paint mixed with sand or a similar abrasive material for the interior surfaces, to provide bats with something to cling onto. Alternatively, you can use plastic mesh or similar materials.

3. Caulk: Silicone caulk to seal edges and joints, helping to weatherproof the bat house and keep it dry inside.

4. Screws: Exterior-grade screws (galvanized or coated) to assemble the bat house securely. The length of the screws will depend on the thickness of your materials but usually, 1 1/2 to 2 inches long screws are suitable.

5. Paint: Water-based, non-toxic paint for the exterior. The color should be chosen based on your climate, with darker colors for cooler regions and lighter colors for warmer regions to help control the internal temperature.

6. Mounting Hardware: Depending on where you plan to install the bat house, you might need brackets, screws, or poles designed for outdoor use.

Tools

1. Saw: A circular saw or handsaw for cutting wood to the desired dimensions.

2. Drill: With a drill bit set for making pilot holes and a screwdriver bit for driving screws.

3. Measuring Tape: To accurately measure and cut wood to the correct sizes.

4. Level : To ensure the bat house is mounted evenly, which is important for stability and water runoff.

5. Caulking Gun: For applying caulk to seams and joints.

6. Paintbrush or Roller: For applying paint to the exterior of the bat house.

7. Sandpaper: To smooth any rough edges on the wood, reducing the risk of injury to bats and to the person handling the bat house.

8. Staple Gun (optional): If using plastic mesh inside the bat house, a staple gun can be used to secure the mesh to the wood.

9. Safety Gear: Safety glasses and gloves to protect yourself while cutting, drilling, and assembling the bat house.

Gathering these materials and tools before you start your project will help ensure a smooth building process. It's also beneficial to have a clear set of instructions or bat house plans to follow, which can provide specific measurements and step-by-step guidance on assembling the bat house correctly. Building a bat house can be a fun and rewarding project, contributing significantly to bat conservation and the health of your local ecosystem.

Bat House Designs and Dimensions

Designing and constructing a bat house requires careful attention to specific designs and dimensions that cater to the needs of bats. These designs are crucial for making the bat house an inviting and suitable habitat for bats to roost, breed, and thrive. The design of a bat house can vary, but there are several key features and dimensions that are essential to include to ensure the bat house is effective.

The internal structure of a bat house is designed to mimic the narrow crevices and spaces that bats prefer for roosting in the wild. This is achieved by creating chambers within the bat house that are tight and dark. The width of these chambers is critical; they should be approximately ¾ inch to 1 inch wide, a size that allows bats to cluster closely for warmth while providing the snug, secure feeling they seek in a roost. Some bat house designs feature multiple chambers, which can make the house more attractive to bats by offering more space and allowing for different temperature gradients within the same structure. Multi-chamber bat houses are generally more successful at attracting bats than single-chamber designs.

The height of the bat house also plays a significant role in its design. A minimum height of 24 inches is recommended, with some designs extending up to 30 or 36 inches. This height provides enough vertical space for bats to move up and down within the house, seeking out areas with the ideal temperature and conditions. The landing area at the bottom of the bat house is another important feature. An extended landing area, typically 3 to 6 inches in height, allows bats easy access to the house and gives young bats a place to land and climb up into the chambers.

The exterior dimensions of the bat house, while somewhat flexible, should be proportionate to support the internal chamber design. A width of 14 to 20 inches is common, providing ample space for a significant number of bats without making the house overly bulky or difficult to mount. The depth of the bat house, measured from the front to the back panel, contributes to the overall interior space and should be sufficient to accommodate the chamber width and insulation, if added, to maintain stable temperatures.

Materials used in the construction of bat houses should be chosen for their durability and suitability for outdoor use. Exterior-grade plywood or cedar are preferred for their resistance to decay. The surface inside the bat house should be rough or grooved to allow bats to grip and cling to the sides easily. This can be achieved through scoring the wood with saw cuts or attaching non-toxic textured materials.

Ventilation is another critical design aspect, especially in warmer climates. Proper ventilation helps to regulate the temperature within the bat house, preventing it from becoming too hot and stifling. This is usually accomplished by incorporating ventilation slots in the design, either on the sides or along the front of the house, just under the roof overhang.

The color and finish of the bat house affect its ability to maintain the right temperature. Darker colors are recommended for cooler climates to help absorb heat, while lighter shades are better suited for warmer regions to reflect sunlight. The paint used should be non-toxic and water-based to avoid harming the bats.

Placement and Installation of Bat Houses

The successful establishment of a bat colony often hinges on the thoughtful placement and installation of bat houses. This involves considering several factors that affect the attractiveness of these artificial roosts to bats, as well as ensuring their longevity and effectiveness as bat habitats. Placement and installation strategies focus on maximizing exposure to essential elements like warmth and providing safety and easy access for bats.

Optimal Placement

Sun Exposure: Bat houses need to receive sufficient sunlight to maintain the warmth required by bats, especially for raising their pups. A minimum of 6 to 8 hours of direct sunlight is recommended. In cooler climates, positioning the bat house to face south or southeast can capture the maximum amount of sunlight. The color of the bat house can also be adjusted according to the climate—darker colors in cooler regions to absorb more heat and lighter shades in warmer areas to reflect sunlight.

Height from Ground: Installing bat houses at least 12 to 20 feet above the ground reduces the risk of predation and increases the likelihood of occupancy by bats. Higher installations, up to about 25 feet, can be even more attractive to bats but must be balanced with the practicality of maintenance and monitoring.

Near Water: Proximity to water sources is a significant attractant for bats, as water bodies support insect populations that serve as food. Ideally, bat houses should be within a quarter mile of a water source, but closer is always better.

Open Flight Path: Bat houses should have clear, unobstructed approaches. This means avoiding dense foliage directly in front of the entrances. A clear flight path enables bats to easily find and access the house without the risk of predation.

Installation Tips

Stable Mounting: Stability is crucial for a bat house. It should not sway in the wind, as this can deter bats from using it. Mounting on a building or a sturdy pole is often more stable than attaching it to a tree. Additionally, trees can provide too much shade and make the bat house accessible to predators.

Avoiding Vibration: Bat houses mounted on poles should be securely fastened to minimize vibration, which can be disturbing to bats. Using a dual-pole mounting system or cross-bracing can add stability.

Maintaining Temperature: The internal temperature of the bat house is critical for bat pup development. Insulating the bat house or using a double-walled design can help regulate temperature, as can adjusting the house's orientation and color based on local climate conditions.

Community Considerations: When installing bat houses in residential areas or public spaces, it's important to consider the human element. Bat houses should not be placed directly over doorways, windows, or frequented areas to avoid potential conflicts. Informing and educating the surrounding community about the benefits of bats and the purpose of the bat houses can foster support and appreciation.

After Installation

Monitoring: After installation, monitoring the bat house for occupancy and condition is important. This helps in understanding bat preferences and can provide insights for future conservation efforts.

Maintenance: Regular checks should be carried out to ensure the bat house remains in good repair and safe for bats. This may involve occasional repainting, clearing of wasp nests, and ensuring the house remains securely mounted.

Patience: It can sometimes take several seasons for bats to discover and start using a new bat house. Patience and persistence, along with adjustments based on observations and learnings, can eventually lead to successful bat house occupation.

Proper placement and installation are critical steps towards creating a welcoming and sustainable environment for bats. By carefully considering these aspects, individuals and communities can significantly contribute to bat conservation and the ecological benefits bats bring.

Height and Orientation

The height and orientation of a bat house are critical factors that significantly influence its attractiveness to bats. Proper attention to these details can enhance the likelihood of bats taking up residence, ensuring the success of your bat conservation efforts.

Height from the Ground

The height at which a bat house is installed affects its thermal regulation, safety from predators, and accessibility to bats. Generally, bat houses should be mounted at least 12 to 20 feet above the ground. This height range discourages predators such as cats and raccoons from accessing the house and provides bats with a sense of security, encouraging them to move in. Additionally, mounting the bat house at this height helps to catch more of the breezes needed for ventilation and cooling during hot weather.

Orientation

The orientation of a bat house is primarily concerned with its exposure to sunlight, as this affects the internal temperature, crucial for the bats' comfort and the rearing of their young. The goal is to maintain an internal temperature between 85°F and 100°F for most bat species during the day, which is essential for pup development.

-Sun Exposure: Bat houses should be oriented to receive maximum sunlight, which typically means facing them south or southeast in northern latitudes to catch the morning sun. In more tropical climates, where overheating could become a problem, slight adjustments might be necessary to avoid the most intense afternoon sun. The specific orientation can depend on local climate conditions, with the aim of achieving the right thermal environment inside the bat house.

-Avoiding Obstructions: The placement should also consider potential obstructions to sunlight, such as buildings or trees, which could cast shadows on the bat house, especially during critical morning hours. Ensuring unobstructed exposure to the sun for most of the day is crucial.

Additional Considerations

- Landscape and Wind: While orienting for optimal sun exposure, consider the landscape and prevailing winds. Bat houses should be placed in locations that are protected from the harshest winds to reduce swaying, which could deter bats. However, some airflow is necessary to prevent the bat house from becoming too stuffy and to aid in temperature regulation.

- View of Surrounding Area: Bats prefer to have a clear view of the surrounding area as they exit their roost. This visibility helps them quickly orient themselves and navigate to foraging sites. Avoid facing the bat house directly towards dense trees or structures that could block this view.

- **Water Proximity:** Orientation towards nearby water sources can also be beneficial, as water attracts insects, providing a feeding area for bats. If possible, the bat house should be placed within a quarter mile of a water body, with the entrance facing the water to make it easier for bats to locate their new home in relation to this essential resource.

Adhering to these guidelines on height and orientation when installing a bat house not only supports the physiological needs of bats but also promotes their safety and reproductive success. By creating an optimally positioned and welcoming environment, you contribute significantly to the conservation of these essential nocturnal creatures and the ecological balance they help maintain.

Temperature and Climate Considerations

Temperature and climate play pivotal roles in the success of a bat house, influencing not only the likelihood of occupancy but also the health and reproductive success of bat residents. Understanding how to manage these factors is crucial for anyone looking to support bat populations effectively.

Temperature Requirements

Bats are highly sensitive to temperature, requiring specific conditions for roosting and breeding. The internal temperature of a bat house is critical, particularly for female bats raising pups. Ideal temperatures typically range from 85°F to 100°F (29°C to 38°C) for most bat species during the maternity season. Achieving and maintaining these temperatures depends on several factors, including the bat house's design, orientation, and the external climate.

Climate Considerations

Design for Climate: The design of a bat house can be tailored to accommodate local climate conditions. In cooler regions, bat houses benefit from being made from darker materials that absorb more heat, thicker walls for insulation, and fewer ventilation openings to retain warmth. In contrast, bat houses in warmer climates should be constructed to enhance ventilation and cooling, using lighter-colored materials to reflect sunlight and prevent overheating.

Orientation: The orientation of a bat house significantly affects its internal temperature. Facing the bat house south or southeast maximizes sun exposure in the northern hemisphere, helping to raise the temperature inside the house. This is particularly important in cooler climates. In hotter regions, a more easterly orientation may prevent the house from getting too hot in the late afternoon.

Sun Exposure: Direct sunlight is crucial for warming up a bat house. Placing the house where it can receive at least six to eight hours of direct sunlight daily is recommended. However, in very hot climates, some afternoon shade might be necessary to prevent overheating.

Ventilation: Proper ventilation helps regulate the temperature within a bat house, preventing it from becoming too hot while still allowing for some warmth retention. Adjustable ventilation, such as sliding panels or removable vents, can offer flexibility in managing internal temperatures throughout different seasons and in varying climates.

Microclimate Creation

Creating a microclimate around the bat house can also help mitigate broader climate impacts. Planting vegetation or installing water features nearby can increase local insect populations, providing a food source for bats while also affecting the microclimate. Strategic placement of plants and water can cool the air in hot climates or shelter the bat house from cold winds in cooler areas.

Monitoring and Adjustment

Monitoring the temperature inside the bat house is key to understanding its suitability for bats. Thermometers or temperature loggers can provide valuable data on the house's internal conditions, indicating whether adjustments are needed. If the bat house is consistently too hot or too cold, repositioning it, altering its orientation, or modifying its design are potential strategies to achieve the optimal temperature range.

Integrating temperature and climate considerations into the planning, design, and placement of bat houses is essential for creating effective and attractive roosting habitats for bats. By carefully managing these elements, conservationists can support the health, reproduction, and long-term viability of bat populations in their local ecosystems.

Attracting Bats to Your Colony

Attracting bats to your colony requires a multifaceted approach that goes beyond just installing bat houses. It involves creating an environment that meets all the needs of bats, including food, water, and shelter, while also considering factors such as safety from predators and minimal human disturbance. Understanding bat behavior and preferences is crucial in making your bat colony an inviting and suitable habitat for these beneficial creatures.

The first step in attracting bats is ensuring that the bat houses are designed, placed, and installed correctly, as detailed in previous discussions. These structures need to be warm enough for bats, especially if they are to be used for rearing young. Achieving the right temperature depends on the climate in your area and the orientation of the bat house. In cooler climates, bat houses should have more sun exposure and possibly darker colors to absorb heat, while in warmer areas, lighter colors and shaded afternoon positions might be necessary to avoid overheating.

The presence of water is a strong attractant for bats. Bats not only need water for drinking but areas around water bodies also tend to have higher insect populations, providing a rich feeding ground. Creating or maintaining water features on your property, such as ponds or water gardens, can enhance the attractiveness of the area to bats. Ensuring these water sources are bat-friendly, with shallow edges or sloped sides for safe access, can further encourage bats to take up residence.

In addition to water, establishing a bat-friendly garden can significantly increase the appeal of your bat colony. Planting night-blooming flowers, native plants, and maintaining areas with natural vegetation can attract insects, providing food for bats. Reducing or eliminating pesticide use in these areas is crucial to ensure that bats have access to a safe and nutritious food supply. Gardens that mimic natural habitats can also provide additional roosting and hiding spots for bats.

Another important aspect of attracting bats is minimizing disturbances and threats from predators. Bats are sensitive to disturbances, especially during their maternity period when females are rearing young. Ensuring that bat houses are placed high enough and in locations that are not easily accessible to predators like cats or raccoons is essential. Similarly, reducing human activity near bat houses, especially during key times such as dusk and dawn when bats are most active, can help make the environment more welcoming.

Engaging with your community can also play a role in attracting bats to your colony. Educating neighbors and the local community about the benefits of bats and how to live harmoniously with them can reduce potential conflicts and create a safer environment for bats. Community-wide efforts to preserve natural areas and reduce pesticide use can further enhance the local ecosystem's attractiveness to bats.

Attracting bats to your colony often requires patience. It may take some time for bats to discover and start using the bat houses. Monitoring bat activity and making adjustments to the bat houses or the surrounding habitat based on observations can improve your chances of success. In some cases, adding bat attractants such as bat guano to or near the bat houses can help, but the effectiveness of this method can vary.

Using Bat Attractants

Using bat attractants is one method to encourage bats to visit and establish colonies in designated bat houses or natural habitats within a particular area. While bats are naturally drawn to environments that meet their essential needs for shelter, food, and water, sometimes additional steps are necessary to make these areas more appealing, especially when trying to establish a new colony. Bat attractants can range from strategic habitat enhancements to the application of specific scents or materials known to be inviting to bats.

The primary and most effective way to attract bats is by creating a habitat that caters to their biological and ecological needs. This involves ensuring that bat houses are properly designed, positioned, and maintained, as discussed in previous sections. Beyond these fundamental requirements, there are additional strategies that can be employed to make an area more attractive to bats.

Enhancing Food Availability

One of the most significant attractants for bats is the availability of food. Many bat species feed on insects, so increasing the insect population around bat houses can make the area more appealing. Planting night-blooming flowers and native plants that attract insects can create a rich feeding ground for bats. Reducing or eliminating the use of pesticides in these areas ensures that bats have access to a safe and nutritious food supply. Gardens that mimic natural habitats not only provide food but also additional roosting and hiding spots for bats, further enhancing the area's attractiveness.

Water Features

Water is a crucial attractant for bats, both for drinking and as a source of insects. Creating or maintaining water features such as ponds, streams, or even birdbaths can draw bats to the area. These water sources should be designed with bat safety in mind, incorporating shallow edges or sloped sides to prevent bats from drowning. The sound of moving water can also attract insects, further increasing the area's appeal to bats.

Mimicking Natural Roost Conditions

Bats are attracted to areas that replicate their natural roosting conditions. This can include the strategic placement of bat houses in locations that offer the optimal temperature, humidity, and security. In some cases, applying bat guano or other organic materials to the inside or entrance of bat houses can make them more inviting. The scent of guano may signal to bats that the house is a suitable roosting site. However, the effectiveness of using guano as an attractant can vary, and it's important to source any such materials responsibly to avoid spreading pathogens.

Minimizing Disturbances

Reducing human activity and noise near bat houses, especially during dusk and dawn when bats are most active, can make the area more welcoming. Bats are more likely to inhabit areas where they feel safe from predators and disturbances. Ensuring that bat houses are placed high enough and in locations that are not easily accessible to predators is essential.

Community Engagement

Engaging with the community to create a bat-friendly environment can also serve as an attractant. Educating neighbors and local communities about the benefits of bats and how to coexist with them harmoniously can reduce potential conflicts and disturbances, making the area more inviting for bats.

Using bat attractants involves a combination of enhancing the natural environment and employing specific strategies to make the area more appealing to bats. While there is no guaranteed method to attract bats immediately, patience and persistence, along with a commitment to creating and maintaining suitable habitats, can eventually lead to the successful establishment of a bat colony.

Managing the Surrounding Environment

Managing the surrounding environment is a pivotal aspect of successfully attracting bats to your colony and ensuring their long-term residence and well-being. This involves creating and maintaining a habitat that supports their natural behaviors and provides them with everything they need to thrive. An effectively managed environment not only benefits bats but also enhances biodiversity and can have positive impacts on the local ecosystem.

Food Sources

One of the key components of managing the surrounding environment is ensuring an ample and ongoing supply of food. For insectivorous bats, this means promoting an ecosystem rich in insects. Planting native vegetation that attracts insects, especially those that are nocturnal pollinators, can significantly increase the food available to bats. Night-blooming flowers, for example, attract night-flying insects that many bat species feed on. Avoiding the use of pesticides is crucial in this effort, as chemicals can reduce insect populations and poison bats. Instead, the presence of bats can serve as a natural pest control method, reducing the need for chemical interventions.

Water Accessibility

Water is another critical resource for bats, both for drinking and as a habitat for insects. Ensuring there are clean, accessible water sources nearby can make the area more attractive to bats. This could involve maintaining natural water bodies, such as ponds or streams, or creating new ones. Adding features that produce gentle noise, like a dripping fountain, can also attract insects, which in turn draw bats.

Shelter and Roosting Sites

Beyond bat houses, maintaining and enhancing natural shelters can provide additional roosting options for bats. This includes preserving old trees, especially those with cavities, and protecting caves or abandoned buildings that bats may use. Ensuring there's a variety of roosting options can cater to different species and their specific needs, increasing the diversity of the bat population in the area.

Safe and Dark Flight Paths

Bats navigate and hunt using echolocation, a process that can be disrupted by excessive light pollution. Keeping the environment around bat colonies as dark as possible during night hours can help bats navigate more effectively and feel safer from predators. This includes minimizing outdoor lighting or opting for bat-friendly lighting options that reduce glare and brightness in key areas.

Natural Vegetation and Landscape

Maintaining a natural and diverse landscape supports a healthy ecosystem that can sustain bats. This involves not only planting trees and shrubs but also preserving underbrush and leaf litter, which can support insect life. Encouraging a variety of plant species can also support a wider range of insects, providing a richer food source for bats.

Community Engagement

Managing the surrounding environment for bats often requires community effort, especially in residential or public areas. Educating the community about the benefits of bats and how to live in harmony with them can lead to broader support for bat-friendly practices. This might include initiatives to reduce pesticide use, protect natural habitats, and minimize light pollution.

Managing the surrounding environment effectively, you create a sustainable ecosystem that supports not only bats but also a wide range of wildlife. This holistic approach to habitat management fosters biodiversity, improves ecological health, and enhances the natural beauty of the area, all while contributing to the conservation of bats.

Water Sources and Bat-Friendly Planting

Integrating water sources and bat-friendly planting into the environment is a strategic approach to attracting and supporting bat populations. These elements cater to the bats' needs for hydration and feeding, creating a hospitable habitat that can encourage bats to take up residence in the area. Implementing these strategies can have a significant positive impact on local bat populations, enhancing biodiversity and promoting ecological balance.

Water Sources

Water is essential for bats, serving both as a drinking source and as a habitat for insects, which are a primary food source for many bat species. Here's how to effectively integrate water sources into your environment:

Creating or Preserving Natural Water Bodies: Natural ponds, streams, and wetlands are ideal for attracting bats due to their role in supporting a diverse insect population. Preserving these natural water bodies and ensuring they remain clean and accessible to bats is crucial.

Installing Artificial Water Features: For areas lacking natural water bodies, installing artificial features like ponds, birdbaths, or even a water garden can provide necessary water sources for bats. Features that mimic natural conditions as closely as possible are preferred.

Ensuring Safe Access: Water features should be designed with shallow edges or include sloped sides to ensure bats can drink safely without the risk of drowning. Smooth surfaces can be difficult for bats to navigate, so adding stones or vegetation at the edges can provide safer landing spots.

Placement: Locating water features near bat houses or known roosting areas can make them more attractive to bats. However, they should be placed in open areas to reduce predation risk while bats are drinking or feeding on insects.

Bat-Friendly Planting

Planting vegetation that attracts insects, especially night-flying species, is another effective way to create a bat-friendly environment.

Here's how to approach bat-friendly planting:

Native Plants: Focusing on native plants is crucial, as these are most likely to support the local insect populations that bats feed on. Native vegetation also requires less maintenance and is more resilient to local pests and diseases.

Night-Blooming Flowers: Including night-blooming flowers in your planting scheme can attract night-flying insects, providing a food source for bats. Flowers like evening primrose, night-scented stock, or moonflower are excellent choices.

Diverse Vegetation: A variety of plants, including trees, shrubs, and ground cover, can support a wider range of insects, offering a more abundant and diverse food source for bats. This diversity also supports other wildlife, contributing to overall ecosystem health.

Pesticide-Free: Maintaining a pesticide-free garden is essential to ensure that insects remain a viable food source for bats. Natural pest control methods, such as encouraging predator insects or using physical barriers, can help manage pest populations without harming bats.

Implementing water sources and bat-friendly planting requires thoughtful planning and ongoing maintenance, but the rewards include a vibrant, biodiverse ecosystem that supports bats and other wildlife. By creating environments that meet the essential needs of bats, you contribute to their conservation and the health of the local ecosystem, showcasing the interdependent nature of our natural world.

Monitoring and Maintenance

Monitoring and maintenance are crucial for the success and longevity of a bat colony, whether it's established in bat houses or natural habitats. These ongoing activities help ensure that the environment remains conducive and safe for bats, allowing for the observation of bat behavior, population changes, and the overall health of the colony. Effective monitoring and maintenance require a thoughtful approach that respects the bats' natural cycles and minimizes disturbances.

Monitoring Efforts

Monitoring involves regularly checking bat houses and natural roosting sites to assess occupancy, health, and any potential issues that may arise. This can include visual inspections to see if bats are using the structures, noting any signs of wear or damage to the houses, and observing bat activity during evening exits. Monitoring should be done with minimal disturbance to the bats, ideally without directly handling them or invading their roosting spaces. The use of technology, such as infrared cameras or bat detectors that record ultrasonic bat calls, can provide insights into bat activity and species presence without interfering with the bats.

Documenting these observations over time creates valuable data that can inform further conservation efforts, help in understanding local bat populations, and guide the refinement of habitat management practices. Regular monitoring schedules should avoid sensitive times such as mating and birthing seasons to prevent stress on the bats.

Maintenance Needs

Maintenance of bat houses and the surrounding habitat is necessary to keep the environment safe and attractive to bats. This might include repairs to the structures to fix wear or damage, ensuring the houses remain securely mounted, and that entrances are clear of obstructions. Over time, bat houses may need to be cleaned or repainted to maintain their structural integrity and appearance, using safe, non-toxic materials that do not harm the bats.

In addition to bat house maintenance, the surrounding habitat should be kept conducive to bat life. This includes managing vegetation to ensure bat houses receive adequate sunlight and maintaining water sources and bat-friendly gardens. Removing or managing threats such as invasive species, predators, or excessive lighting is also part of ongoing maintenance efforts.

Ethical Considerations

Throughout the monitoring and maintenance processes, ethical considerations must be at the forefront. Disturbing bats, especially during critical times like hibernation or when rearing young, can have negative impacts on their health and stress levels. Activities should be planned around the bats' schedules, and any necessary interventions should be as non-invasive as possible.

Community Involvement

Engaging the community in monitoring and maintenance activities can foster a greater appreciation for bats and their ecological roles. Educational programs, citizen science projects, and volunteer opportunities can help spread awareness and encourage collective efforts in bat conservation. Community involvement can also lead to broader support for habitat protection and enhancement initiatives.

Professional Assistance

For certain aspects of monitoring and maintenance, especially when dealing with large colonies, health concerns, or significant habitat restoration projects, consulting with wildlife professionals or bat conservation organizations can provide expertise and guidance.

These experts can offer advice on best practices, assist with health assessments, and help address any complex issues that arise.

Regular monitoring and maintenance are foundational to the success of a bat colony. These practices ensure that habitats remain safe, attractive, and conducive to the bats' needs, facilitating their conservation and the health of local ecosystems. Through careful planning, ethical consideration, and community engagement, the long-term well-being of bat populations can be supported, contributing to biodiversity and natural pest control benefits.

Regular Checks and Maintenance of Bat Houses

Regular checks and maintenance of bat houses are essential to ensure they remain safe, attractive, and functional habitats for bats. These activities not only help in sustaining the bat population in the area but also in monitoring the health and success of the bat colony. Here's a deeper dive into the processes involved in the regular checks and maintenance of bat houses:

Timing and Frequency

The timing of checks should be planned to minimize disturbance to bats. Ideally, inspections should occur during times when bats are least likely to be in the houses, such as late fall or winter in temperate regions, when bats have migrated or are hibernating elsewhere. However, a preliminary check in early spring can be beneficial to assess the bat house after the winter and prepare for the bats' return. The frequency of these checks should be balanced to monitor the condition and occupancy without causing undue stress to the bats; once or twice a year is typically sufficient.

Inspection Checklist

During an inspection, several aspects of the bat house should be examined:

Structural Integrity: Check for any signs of wear, damage, or deterioration. This includes loose panels or screws, cracks in the wood, and the stability of the mount. The bat house must remain securely attached to its support structure, whether a pole, tree, or building.

Entrance and Interior: Ensure the entrance is clear of obstructions and that the interior spaces are intact. Over time, the entrance may become clogged with debris or the interior surfaces worn smooth, making it difficult for bats to grip.

Moisture and Ventilation: Look for signs of water damage or excessive moisture inside the bat house, which can lead to mold growth. Ventilation slots should be clear to allow for proper air flow, preventing the interior from becoming too hot or humid.

Signs of Occupancy: Look for indications that bats are using the house, such as guano beneath the entrance or staining around the entrance hole. Presence of insects or birds nesting in the bat house should be noted, as they may deter bats from moving in.

Maintenance Actions

Following the inspection, any identified issues should be addressed promptly:

Repairs: Fix any structural problems, securing loose panels or replacing damaged parts. Ensure the bat house remains stable and secure against winds and weather.

Cleaning: Remove any blockages at the entrance. While bat houses typically do not require interior cleaning, if pests or mold are found, seeking advice from a bat conservation organization on safe cleaning methods is recommended.

Surface Renewal: If the interior surfaces have become too smooth, roughening them up again can make the house more usable for bats. This might involve adding non-toxic, water-based paint mixed with sand to create texture or affixing safe, rough materials to the interior.

Repositioning: If the bat house has not been occupied for several years, consider moving it to a new location that might be more attractive to bats, based on sun exposure, height, and proximity to water and food sources.

Recoating: Apply a fresh coat of non-toxic, water-based paint on the exterior if necessary to maintain the bat house's temperature regulation properties, based on the climate and orientation.

Documentation: Keeping records of each inspection and maintenance activity, including the condition of the bat house, any repairs made, and signs of occupancy, can be valuable. This documentation can help track the success of the bat house over time, identify patterns in bat behavior or preferences, and provide insights for future bat house projects.

Regular checks and maintenance of bat houses are key to fostering a healthy and successful bat colony. By ensuring the bat houses remain in good condition, you can support the conservation of bats and benefit from their presence in the ecosystem.

Data Collection and Monitoring Bat Activity

Data collection and monitoring bat activity are integral components of managing a successful bat colony. These processes provide valuable insights into the behaviors, preferences, and health of bat populations, enabling more informed conservation efforts and habitat management. Through systematic observation and recording, one can gauge the success of bat houses, understand seasonal changes in bat activity, and identify potential threats or challenges facing the colony.

The cornerstone of data collection is establishing a baseline of bat activity before and after the installation of bat houses or the enhancement of natural habitats. This involves noting the number of bats present, species identification if possible, and their behavior patterns. Monitoring tools and methods vary in complexity from simple visual observations to the use of advanced technological equipment.

Visual observation remains one of the most accessible and commonly used methods for monitoring bat activity. This includes watching for bats at dusk and dawn when they are most active, noting their exit and return to the bat houses, and any social behaviors observed. Such observations can be complemented with regular inspections of the bat houses for signs of occupancy, such as the presence of guano beneath roosting sites or staining from bat oils near entry points.

For more detailed monitoring, acoustic detectors can be employed. These devices record ultrasonic bat calls, which are beyond the range of human hearing. The data collected can then be analyzed to identify species, estimate population sizes, and study bat activity patterns. Acoustic monitoring provides a non-invasive means to gather detailed information about bat communities over time.

Photographic and video recordings can also be valuable tools for monitoring bat activity. Cameras, especially those with night vision or infrared capabilities, can capture bats' nocturnal behaviors without disturbing them. This method allows for the documentation of bats entering and exiting bat houses, interacting with each other, and can even help in identifying predators or competitors that may threaten the bat colony.

Environmental data should also be collected to understand better the conditions that affect bat activity. This includes temperature and humidity levels inside and outside bat houses, weather conditions, and lunar phases. Such environmental factors can significantly influence bat behaviors and preferences, and tracking these alongside bat activity can reveal important correlations.

Data collection and monitoring should be conducted regularly and over extended periods to capture seasonal variations in bat activity and long-term trends in population dynamics. However, it is crucial to balance the need for information with the well-being of the bats, ensuring that monitoring methods are as non-intrusive as possible.

The data gathered through these monitoring efforts should be systematically recorded and analyzed. Keeping detailed records allows for the assessment of the success of habitat management strategies, the identification of emerging threats, and the formulation of responses to any changes in bat activity or health. Sharing findings with the broader scientific and conservation communities can also contribute to the collective knowledge about bats and support global conservation efforts.

In summary, data collection and monitoring bat activity are essential for understanding and supporting bat colonies. Through careful observation and the use of technology, valuable data can be gathered, contributing to the conservation of these important creatures and the ecosystems they inhabit.

Troubleshooting Common Issues

In the process of establishing and maintaining a bat colony, several common issues may arise that require troubleshooting. These challenges can range from a lack of bat occupancy in provided houses to managing the impact of bats on human communities. Addressing these issues effectively is crucial for the success of bat conservation efforts and ensuring coexistence between bats and humans.

One frequent concern is bats not occupying bat houses. Several factors could contribute to this issue, including the location, design, and conditions of the bat houses. Ensuring the houses are placed in areas with adequate sun exposure, away from predators, and at the correct height can make them more attractive to bats. Additionally, the interior of the bat house should be designed to mimic natural roosting conditions closely, with appropriate textures and temperatures. If bats still do not occupy the houses after one or two seasons, it may be necessary to reevaluate the location and design, possibly relocating the houses to a more suitable area.

Another issue can arise from bat guano accumulation beneath roosting sites. While guano is beneficial for gardens as a fertilizer, excessive accumulation can become a nuisance and health concern. Regular cleaning and the installation of guano collection trays can help manage this issue. It's also possible to landscape the area under bat houses with gravel or similar materials that make cleaning easier and reduce the impact on the ground below.

Conflicts with human residents can occur, particularly when bats inadvertently enter living spaces or when there is concern about diseases. Educating the community about the benefits of bats, the low risk of disease transmission, and how to safely coexist with bats can alleviate many concerns. Providing information on sealing entry points to prevent bats from entering buildings, while ensuring they can still access outdoor roosting sites, can help manage cohabitation issues.

Predation by cats and other animals is a risk to bat populations, especially when bats are entering or exiting roosting sites. Installing bat houses away from trees and structures that predators can climb, and keeping domestic cats indoors during dusk and dawn when bats are most active, can reduce predation risks.

Sometimes, bat houses may attract unwanted guests, such as wasps or bees. This can deter bats from using the houses. Monitoring for signs of these unwanted occupants and carefully removing them during periods when bats are not present can help keep the houses ready for bat occupancy. It's essential to approach this task with caution and consider consulting professionals for safe removal, especially in the case of bees, which are valuable pollinators.

Weather and environmental conditions can also affect bat houses, such as extreme temperatures or water leakage. Ensuring that bat houses are built with durable materials and designed to withstand local weather conditions is critical. This might include adding ventilation slots to improve air circulation during hot weather or ensuring the houses are waterproof and insulated against cold temperatures.

Troubleshooting common issues in bat conservation efforts involves a combination of proactive design and placement of bat houses, regular maintenance, community education, and addressing specific challenges as they arise. Through careful management and a willingness to adapt strategies based on observation and experience, it is possible to support healthy bat colonies and foster a positive relationship between bats and humans.

Engaging the Community

Engaging the community in bat conservation efforts is a vital strategy for ensuring the success and sustainability of bat colonies. Community involvement not only helps in garnering support and understanding for bats but also plays a significant role in creating a more inclusive and informed approach to environmental stewardship. By engaging a diverse range of stakeholders, from local residents and schools to businesses and governmental agencies, conservation efforts can benefit from a broader base of knowledge, resources, and enthusiasm.

The first step in engaging the community is often education. Dispelling myths and misconceptions about bats is crucial, as fear and misunderstanding can hinder conservation efforts. Educational programs, workshops, and informative materials can introduce community members to the ecological benefits of bats, such as their roles in pest control and pollination. Highlighting the fascinating aspects of bat biology and behavior can also spark interest and appreciation.

Schools offer a particularly effective avenue for community engagement. Incorporating bat education into science curricula or after-school programs can foster early interest in conservation. Projects such as building bat houses or creating bat-friendly gardens provide hands-on learning opportunities and can instill a sense of responsibility towards local ecosystems.

Community events centered around bats, such as bat walks, talks by bat experts, or bat house building workshops, can further raise awareness and interest. These events provide platforms for direct engagement, allowing community members to ask questions, share experiences, and learn from one another. They can also serve as opportunities to involve the community in ongoing monitoring and data collection efforts, turning bat conservation into a citizen science project.

Partnerships with local businesses and organizations can enhance community engagement efforts by providing resources, funding, or platforms for outreach. Businesses can sponsor bat conservation projects or participate in adopt-a-bat house programs. Collaborations with environmental organizations can offer expertise and additional educational resources.

Engaging with local government and planning bodies is also important. Advocating for bat-friendly policies, such as reducing light pollution or protecting natural habitats, can have a significant impact on the broader environment in which bats live. This level of engagement requires building relationships with policymakers and participating in planning processes, highlighting the importance of bats to healthy ecosystems.

Throughout all these efforts, communication is key. Regular updates on the status of local bat colonies, successes in bat house occupation, or interesting findings from monitoring efforts can keep the community informed and invested. Social media, local news outlets, and community bulletin boards can all serve as platforms for sharing stories and updates.

Engaging the community in bat conservation is about building relationships and fostering a collective sense of stewardship. By involving a wide range of participants, from children learning about bats for the first time to policymakers who can effect change on a larger scale, conservation efforts can achieve greater impact. This holistic approach not only benefits bats but also enriches the community, enhancing local biodiversity and promoting a healthier, more sustainable relationship with the natural world.

Educating Neighbors and Local Communities

Engaging and educating neighbors and local communities about bats is a vital step towards fostering a supportive environment for bat conservation efforts. This process involves dispelling myths, highlighting the ecological benefits of bats, and encouraging community participation in bat-friendly practices. Through education, communities can become allies in the conservation of bats, contributing to the broader goals of biodiversity preservation and ecological health.

Starting with informative sessions can lay the groundwork for community engagement. These sessions can cover a range of topics, including the vital roles bats play in ecosystems, such as pest control, pollination, and seed dispersal. Many people are unaware that bats are responsible for billions of dollars' worth of pest control in agriculture annually or that they contribute to the reproduction of many plants. Presenting facts and figures can help illustrate the importance of bats beyond their immediate ecosystem.

Addressing common misconceptions about bats is another crucial aspect of community education. Many fears surrounding bats are based on myths or misinformation, such as the belief that all bats carry rabies. While bats can carry diseases, the risk of transmission to humans is extremely low, especially if direct contact is avoided. Educating the community on safe practices for coexisting with bats, such as not handling bats and securing homes against unwanted bat entry, can mitigate concerns and promote cohabitation.

Community education efforts can also extend to schools, local clubs, and organizations, where interactive presentations, bat house building workshops, and bat watching events can engage a wider audience. Involving children and youth in bat conservation projects not only educates them but also instills a sense of stewardship for local wildlife and the environment from a young age.

Creating informative materials such as brochures, websites, or social media pages dedicated to local bat conservation can provide ongoing resources for the community. These materials can offer tips on how to attract bats, how to build and where to place bat houses, and how to participate in citizen science projects that monitor bat populations.

Collaboration with local environmental groups, wildlife agencies, and bat conservation organizations can amplify educational efforts. These partnerships can bring in experts for talks, provide educational materials, and support community-led conservation projects. They can also offer a channel for community concerns to be addressed by professionals, further building trust and support for bat conservation.

Community education is not just about disseminating information; it's also about listening to community concerns, questions, and suggestions. Open dialogues can lead to more effective and inclusive conservation strategies that consider both human and wildlife needs. Encouraging community feedback and participation in decision-making processes can foster a sense of ownership and responsibility towards local conservation efforts.

Collaboration with Local Wildlife Organizations

Collaboration with local wildlife organizations plays a pivotal role in the successful conservation and understanding of bat populations. These partnerships can provide a wealth of knowledge, resources, and support, making them indispensable for individuals and communities engaged in bat conservation efforts. By working together, the collective impact on bat preservation can be significantly amplified, leading to more effective and sustainable conservation outcomes.

Local wildlife organizations, including environmental groups, bat conservation societies, and governmental wildlife agencies, possess extensive expertise in regional biodiversity, ecosystem management, and species-specific conservation strategies. Their experience with local wildlife laws, habitat requirements, and conservation challenges can guide the development of effective bat conservation projects, ensuring they align with broader environmental goals and comply with legal requirements.

One of the primary benefits of collaborating with these organizations is access to expert guidance. Specialists in bat ecology can offer advice on designing and placing bat houses, restoring natural habitats, and best practices for monitoring and maintaining bat colonies. They can also assist in identifying bat species, understanding their behaviors, and addressing any health issues or risks that may arise.

Educational outreach is another area where local wildlife organizations can make a significant contribution. They often have resources, such as informational materials, speakers, and workshop programs that can be utilized to educate the community about the importance of bats. These resources can help dispel myths and fears surrounding bats, highlighting their role in pest control, pollination, and maintaining healthy ecosystems.

Moreover, collaboration with wildlife organizations can enhance data collection and research efforts. Many organizations conduct studies on bat populations, migration patterns, and health issues, such as white-nose syndrome. Participating in these research efforts by sharing data from local bat colonies can contribute valuable insights to the scientific community, aiding in the conservation of bats on a larger scale.

Collaborating on conservation projects can also lead to increased funding and resource availability. Many wildlife organizations have access to grants and funding opportunities specifically aimed at conservation projects. By partnering on initiatives, it's possible to pool resources, share costs, and achieve more ambitious conservation goals than might be feasible independently.

Community engagement and advocacy are further strengthened through collaboration with wildlife organizations. These groups often have established networks and platforms for raising awareness and advocating for policy changes beneficial to wildlife conservation. Joining forces can amplify the message, reaching a wider audience and garnering support for bat conservation efforts.

Organizing Bat Watching Events

Organizing bat watching events is a fantastic way to engage the community, raise awareness about bat conservation, and foster a deeper appreciation for these often misunderstood creatures. Such events can serve as both educational experiences and enjoyable community activities, offering participants the chance to observe bats in their natural environment and learn about their behaviors and ecological benefits.

Here's a detailed look at how to plan and execute a successful bat watching event:

Planning the Event

Choosing the Location: Select a location known for bat activity, ideally near a bat colony, water body, or a feeding site. Parks, nature reserves, and areas near bat houses are excellent choices. Ensure the site is accessible and safe for participants of all ages.

Timing: Schedule the event around dusk or early evening, which is when bats are most active. Consider the time of year as well; late spring through early fall is usually when bats are most visible in temperate climates.

Permissions and Safety: Obtain any necessary permissions from local authorities or landowners. Plan for the safety of participants by checking the site for hazards, arranging for first aid on site, and considering any local wildlife that might be encountered.

Collaboration: Partnering with local wildlife organizations, bat conservation groups, or naturalists can enhance the event with expert knowledge and additional resources. These experts can provide insights into bat behavior, identification, and conservation efforts.

Promoting the Event

Community Outreach: Use local community boards, social media, school groups, and environmental organizations to spread the word. Clear communication about the purpose, timing, and location of the event, as well as what participants can expect, is key.

Educational Materials: Prepare or source educational materials to distribute at the event. This could include brochures about local bat species, their ecological roles, and how to support bat conservation at home.

During the Event

Welcome and Introduction: Start with a brief welcome and introduction, outlining the schedule for the event. Introduce any bat experts or speakers who will be sharing information.

Educational Presentation: Before heading out to watch bats, a short presentation can provide valuable background information. Topics might include bat ecology, the importance of bats in pest control, myths about bats, and how to observe bats respectfully.

Guided Observation: Lead participants to the observation area and guide them on how to spot bats. Using bat detectors can enrich the experience by converting bat echolocation calls into audible sounds, helping participants locate and identify different species.

Interactive Activities: Depending on the audience, include interactive elements such as bat-themed games for children, Q&A sessions with experts, or citizen science projects like bat call recording.

Follow-up: Encourage participants to share their experiences and photos from the event on social media or with the organizing groups. Provide information on how they can continue to support bat conservation efforts.

After the Event

Feedback: Collect feedback from participants to understand what worked well and what could be improved for future events. This can help in refining the approach and making bat watching events even more engaging and informative.

Continued Engagement: Keep participants engaged with follow-up information, additional resources, or notifications about future events. Building a community interested in bat conservation can have lasting positive impacts on local bat populations and broader environmental awareness.

Organizing bat watching events requires careful planning and a passion for sharing the wonders of the natural world with others. By providing an opportunity for direct engagement with wildlife, such events can transform perceptions, inspire conservation action, and cultivate a community of bat advocates.

Conservation and Beyond

Conservation and beyond encompasses a broad vision for protecting bats and their habitats while promoting a sustainable coexistence between humans and the natural world. This holistic approach not only focuses on the immediate needs of bat conservation, such as habitat protection and restoration but also looks forward to fostering an ecosystem where bats can thrive in harmony with human activities. It involves a multifaceted strategy that integrates research, community engagement, policy advocacy, and educational initiatives to create a lasting impact on bat populations and the broader environment.

At the heart of bat conservation is the understanding of bats' ecological roles. Bats are essential for healthy ecosystems, contributing to pest control, pollination, and seed dispersal. Recognizing these contributions highlights the importance of bats beyond their immediate environments, linking their well-being to broader ecological and economic benefits. Conservation efforts, therefore, aim to protect and restore natural habitats, such as forests, caves, and wet-lands that are crucial for bat foraging, roosting, and breeding.

Beyond habitat preservation, addressing threats to bat populations is critical. This includes combating issues like white-nose syndrome, a devastating disease affecting hibernating bats; mitigating bat fatalities at wind turbines; and reducing the impact of pesticides and habitat fragmentation. Research and monitoring play key roles in understanding these threats and devising effective mitigation strategies. Citizen science projects can also contribute valuable data on bat populations and health, engaging the public in conservation efforts.

Engaging communities in bat conservation is fundamental, by educating people about the benefits of bats and dispelling myths that foster fear and misunderstanding, conservation programs can cultivate a more bat-friendly society. This involves not just sharing knowledge but also listening to and addressing community concerns, creating partnerships that benefit both people and bats. Community-based initiatives, such as bat house projects and habitat restoration efforts, empower local stakeholders to take an active role in conservation.

Policy advocacy is another crucial element, Working with lawmakers and regulatory bodies to enact and enforce legislation that protects bats and their habitats ensures that conservation efforts are supported at all levels of government. This can include policies on land use, wildlife protection, and environmental impact assessments for development projects. Conservation groups can collaborate with policymakers to draft bat-friendly regulations and ensure that bats are considered in broader environmental and land management policies.

Looking beyond immediate conservation needs, fostering a culture that values and protects biodiversity is essential for the long-term well-being of bat populations. This includes promoting sustainable land use practices, supporting organic farming methods that reduce pesticide use, and encouraging urban planning that incorporates green spaces and wildlife corridors. By integrating bat conservation into broader environmental and sustainability efforts, the goal is to create landscapes where bats and humans can thrive together.

Conservation and beyond envisions a future where bats are recognized and valued for their contributions to the natural world and human well-being. Through collaborative efforts that combine research, education, community engagement, and policy advocacy, it's possible to create a more sustainable and bat-friendly world. This holistic approach not only benefits bats but also contributes to the health and resilience of ecosystems worldwide, ensuring a richer, more biodiverse planet for future generations.

Contributing to Bat Conservation Efforts

Contributing to bat conservation efforts is a multifaceted endeavor that can involve individuals, communities, and organizations in activities ranging from habitat preservation to public education. The decline in bat populations globally due to habitat loss, climate change, disease, and other factors makes such efforts more critical than ever. Here's a deeper exploration into how contributions can be made to support bat conservation:

Habitat Preservation and Restoration

Protecting and restoring bat habitats is fundamental. This can involve participating in or supporting reforestation projects, protecting existing forests and waterways, and restoring natural habitats that have been degraded. Simple actions like planting native vegetation in your garden or community spaces can create more foraging opportunities for bats. On a larger scale, advocating for the protection of critical bat habitats, such as caves, old-growth forests, and wetlands, through support of conservation organizations or participation in public land use planning processes, can contribute significantly to the preservation of bat populations.

Building and Installing Bat Houses

One of the most direct ways individuals and communities can contribute to bat conservation is by building and installing bat houses. Providing safe roosting spaces can help local bat populations thrive, especially in areas where natural roosts have been lost. Bat house projects can also serve as educational tools, raising awareness about bats and their needs. Participating in workshops or organizing bat house building events can engage a wider audience in conservation efforts.

Citizen Science

Participation in citizen science projects offers valuable support to bat conservation by gathering data on bat populations, behaviors, and health. This can involve monitoring bat houses, recording bat calls, or participating in surveys and counts. The data collected through citizen science projects can help researchers track trends in bat populations, understand the impacts of threats, and develop effective conservation strategies. Engaging in these projects not only contributes valuable information but also increases public understanding and appreciation of bats.

Advocacy and Policy Support

Advocating for policies that protect bats and their habitats is another critical area of contribution. This can include writing to local representatives, participating in public meetings, and supporting conservation organizations in their policy efforts. Advocacy can also involve raising awareness about the challenges facing bats, such as the need for greener pest management practices that reduce pesticide use, the protection of key habitats from development, and the implementation of wildlife-friendly farming and forestry practices.

Education and Outreach

Educating others about the importance of bats and the challenges they face is essential for building broad support for conservation efforts. This can be done through informal discussions, presentations at schools or community groups, social media, and support of bat conservation organizations' outreach programs. Dispelling myths and misconceptions about bats can change public perceptions, leading to greater tolerance and support for bats in local communities.

Financial Support

Donating to organizations dedicated to bat conservation supports research, habitat protection, and education programs directly. Financial contributions can help fund critical projects, from disease research and monitoring equipment to conservation education programs and advocacy efforts. Supporting bat conservation organizations through memberships or adopting a bat are additional ways to provide financial assistance.

Volunteering

Volunteering time with conservation organizations, whether through hands-on habitat restoration projects, educational outreach, or administrative support, is invaluable. Volunteering can also provide personal growth opportunities, such as learning more about bats and conservation practices, gaining new skills, and connecting with others who share a passion for wildlife and the environment.

Contributing to bat conservation efforts requires a comprehensive approach that includes habitat protection, education, advocacy, and research support.

Expanding Your Bat Colony

Expanding your bat colony can be a rewarding endeavor, contributing significantly to local biodiversity and the broader ecosystem. As bat populations face various threats, efforts to support and increase their numbers are vital. Expansion involves creating additional habitats, enhancing food sources, and ensuring the colony's long-term sustainability. Here's how you can go about expanding your bat colony effectively:

Add More Bat Houses

Introducing additional bat houses is a straightforward method to accommodate a growing bat population. When adding new houses, consider different designs and sizes to cater to various species and their roosting preferences. Placement is key—ensure new bat houses are located near existing ones but also explore new areas that could be attractive to bats, based on their access to water, food, and flight paths. Installing bat houses at different orientations can also help accommodate temperature preferences throughout the seasons.

Improve Habitat Quality

Enhancing the quality of the surrounding habitat can support a larger bat population by providing ample food and water. This might involve planting a diversity of native plants to attract insects, creating or restoring water features, and maintaining areas of natural vegetation that offer foraging opportunities. Additionally, managing the landscape to reduce pesticide use and protect natural insect populations is crucial.

Connect Habitats

Creating habitat corridors can facilitate bat movement across larger areas, connecting isolated populations and expanding their range. This can involve planting tree lines or hedgerows and restoring natural landscapes that allow bats to safely travel between roosting and foraging sites. Efforts to connect habitats also help in genetic diversity, making bat populations more resilient.

Foster Community Involvement

Engaging the community in bat conservation efforts can multiply the impact of your actions. Educating neighbors and local communities about the benefits of bats, how to create bat-friendly environments, and the importance of habitat connectivity encourages broader participation. Community-wide initiatives, such as group bat house building projects or habitat restoration days, can foster a supportive environment for bats.

Monitor and Adapt

Continuously monitoring the bat colony and the effectiveness of new habitats is important for understanding the needs of your growing bat population. This can involve regular observations of bat house occupancy, bat activity in the area, and the condition of the habitats. Be prepared to adapt your strategies based on what you learn. For example, if certain bat houses remain unoccupied or if bats show a preference for specific areas, this information can guide future expansion efforts.

Collaborate with Conservation Organizations

Working with bat conservation organizations can provide valuable insights and resources for expanding your bat colony. These organizations can offer advice on bat house placement, habitat management, and can assist in monitoring efforts. Collaboration might also open up opportunities for participating in larger conservation projects that benefit bats on a regional scale.

Ensure Legal Compliance

As you plan to expand your bat colony, ensure your efforts comply with local wildlife protection laws and regulations. Some bat species are protected, and specific actions may be required to support their conservation legally. Consulting with wildlife agencies can provide guidance and ensure your conservation activities are beneficial and compliant. Expanding your bat colony not only helps protect these essential creatures but also contributes to the health of local ecosystems.

Resources and Further Reading

For those interested in delving deeper into bat conservation, understanding bats, and enhancing bat habitats, a wealth of resources and literature is available to guide, educate, and inspire. These resources range from scientific research articles and conservation guidelines to practical guides for building bat houses and engaging communities in bat conservation efforts. Here is an overview of the types of resources and suggestions for further reading that can provide valuable insights and support for anyone looking to contribute to the well-being of bats.

Scientific Journals and Articles

Academic journals such as "Journal of Bat Research & Conservation" and "Acta Chiropterologica" publish peer-reviewed articles on bat biology, ecology, and conservation. These publications are excellent for those looking for in-depth research findings, case studies, and reviews of current knowledge on various aspects of bat conservation.

Books

Several comprehensive books have been written on bats, offering insights into their behavior, ecological roles, and conservation. Titles like "Bats in the Anthropocene: Conservation of Bats in a Changing World" edited by Christian C. Voigt and Tigga Kingston, and "America's Neighborhood Bats" by Merlin Tuttle provide valuable information and are accessible to both scientific and general audiences.

Conservation Organizations

Organizations dedicated to bat conservation, such as Bat Conservation International, The Bat Conservation Trust (UK), and Bat Conservation Africa, offer a plethora of online resources. These include guidelines for bat house construction, tips for creating bat-friendly gardens, and educational materials on the importance of bats. These organizations' websites also often feature news, updates on conservation projects, and opportunities for public participation and support.

Government and Wildlife Agencies

Many governmental wildlife agencies provide resources on local bat species, habitat conservation guidelines, and legal aspects of bat protection. For example, the U.S. Fish and Wildlife Service and the Natural Resources Conservation Service offer publications and online resources that can be instrumental for those involved in land management or looking to contribute to bat conservation on their property.

Online Forums and Social Media

Online forums and social media groups dedicated to bat conservation and wildlife gardening can be excellent sources of practical advice, support, and inspiration. These platforms allow for the exchange of experiences and tips among enthusiasts and experts, making them valuable resources for troubleshooting and innovative conservation strategies.

Workshops and Webinars

Attending workshops and webinars hosted by conservation organizations, wildlife agencies, or academic institutions can provide hands-on learning opportunities and up-to-date information on bat conservation. These events often cover a range of topics, from the basics of bat ecology to advanced conservation techniques.

Citizen Science Projects

Participation in citizen science projects can be both a learning experience and a way to contribute valuable data to bat conservation. Projects like Bat Watch, iNaturalist, and the North American Bat Monitoring Program (NABat) allow individuals to get involved in monitoring bat populations and submitting observations.

Educational Videos and Documentaries

Visual media such as documentaries and online videos can offer engaging introductions to the world of bats. Platforms like YouTube host a variety of educational content produced by wildlife experts, conservation organizations, and enthusiasts, providing insights into bat behavior, conservation challenges, and success stories.

Expanding one's knowledge through these resources and further reading can deepen understanding, foster a greater appreciation for bats, and inspire more effective conservation actions. Whether you are a novice looking to learn about bats, an educator seeking materials for instruction, or a conservationist in search of advanced strategies for habitat management, the wealth of available information can support your journey in bat conservation.

Frequently Asked Questions (FAQ)

Creating a Frequently Asked Questions (FAQ) section about starting and maintaining a bat colony provides a valuable resource for addressing common queries and concerns. This resource can help dispel myths, educate, and encourage best practices among those interested in bat conservation.

Here are detailed answers to some commonly asked questions:

Can I attract bats to my yard?

Yes, you can attract bats to your yard by providing suitable habitats such as bat houses, ensuring there are water sources nearby, and maintaining a garden that attracts insects for bats to feed on. Avoiding pesticides and creating a night-friendly environment by minimizing outdoor lighting can also make your yard more inviting to bats.

Are bats dangerous to have around?

Bats are generally not dangerous and play vital roles in ecosystems, such as controlling insect populations and pollinating plants. While some bats can carry diseases like rabies, the risk of transmission to humans is very low, especially if you avoid handling bats. With proper education and precautions, the benefits of having bats nearby far outweigh the risks.

How long does it take for bats to move into a new bat house?

The time it takes for bats to occupy a new bat house can vary widely; some houses are occupied within a few months, while others may take a couple of years or more. Factors influencing occupancy include the bat house design, placement, the local bat population, and the availability of suitable natural habitats. Patience is key, and sometimes minor adjustments to the placement or orientation of the bat house can help.

How do I know if bats are using the bat house?

Signs that bats are using a bat house include seeing bats enter or exit the house around dusk or dawn, spotting bat guano (droppings) beneath the house, and observing staining from the oils in bat fur near the entrance. You might also hear the bats' chirping sounds on quiet evenings.

What should I do if a bat gets inside my home?

If a bat gets inside your home, the best approach is to isolate the bat in one room (if possible) by closing doors to other parts of the house. Open windows and exterior doors in the room where the bat is to give it a chance to exit on its own. Avoid direct contact with the bat. If the bat does not leave on its own, contact local wildlife control or a bat conservation organization for assistance in safely removing the bat.

How can I help support bat conservation?

Supporting bat conservation can be done in several ways: installing bat houses, participating in or donating to bat conservation organizations, engaging in citizen science projects to help monitor bat populations, educating others about the importance of bats, and advocating for the protection of natural bat habitats. Every action, no matter how small, contributes to the overall effort to conserve bat populations.

Do bat houses require maintenance?

Yes, bat houses require periodic checks and maintenance to ensure they remain safe and attractive to bats. This includes inspecting the house for structural integrity, ensuring it is securely mounted, checking for signs of occupancy, and occasionally cleaning out any pests that may have taken residence. Maintenance should be carried out carefully to avoid disturbing any bats that might be using the house.

Addressing these FAQs provides a starting point for individuals and communities interested in bat conservation, offering guidance and encouragement for those looking to make a positive impact on local bat populations and ecosystems.

Glossary

This glossary is for terms related to bat conservation and the establishment of bat colonies can clarify concepts and enhance understanding for individuals interested in these topics.

Here's a detailed glossary of terms:

Bat Conservation

The act of protecting and supporting bat populations and their habitats, through various efforts such as habitat restoration, research, public education, and policy advocacy, to ensure their survival and well-being.

Bat House

A man-made structure designed to provide bats with a safe place to roost, breed, and raise their young. These houses mimic the crevices and cavities that bats naturally seek for shelter.

Echolocation

A biological sonar used by bats (and some other animals) to navigate and locate prey in the dark. Bats emit ultrasonic sounds that bounce off objects and return as echoes, allowing them to "see" their surroundings through sound.

Habitat

The natural environment in which a species lives and grows. For bats, this includes roosting sites (such as caves, trees, or bat houses), water sources, and foraging areas rich in insects.

Hibernacula

Plural of hibernaculum, which refers to the places where bats hibernate during the winter. These are typically caves or mines that maintain stable, cool temperatures that allow bats to slow their metabolism and conserve energy.

Insectivorous

Referring to animals that primarily feed on insects. Many bat species are insectivorous and play a crucial role in controlling pest populations.

Maternity Colony

A group of female bats that come together in a specific location to give birth and raise their young. These colonies are important for the survival of bat populations, providing a safe environment for pups to grow until they can fly and forage on their own.

Microhabitat

A small or specialized habitat within a larger ecosystem that supports specific species due to its unique conditions, such as temperature, humidity, and shelter.

Nocturnal

Animals that are active during the night and rest during the day. Most bat species are nocturnal, hunting for insects and engaging in other activities under the cover of darkness.

Pollination

The process of transferring pollen from the male parts of a flower to the female parts, facilitating the fertilization and production of seeds. Some bat species are important pollinators for certain plants and crops.

Roost

The place where bats rest, sleep, or reside. Roosts can be found in natural settings like caves and trees or in man-made structures such as bat houses and buildings.

Ultrasonic

Sound waves with frequencies higher than the upper audible limit of human hearing. Bats use ultrasonic sounds for echolocation, which are beyond the range of what humans can hear without special equipment.

This glossary provides a foundational understanding of terms related to bat conservation and the creation and management of bat colonies. It serves as a resource for education and awareness, helping to demystify the scientific and ecological aspects of bat conservation efforts.

Definitions of Terms Related to Bats and Bat Conservation

Understanding the terms related to bats and bat conservation is essential for anyone involved in or interested in the protection and study of these important creatures.

Here are definitions for key terms:

Biodiversity: The variety of life in the world or in a particular habitat or ecosystem. Bats contribute to biodiversity by fulfilling many ecological roles, such as pollinators, seed dispersers, and natural pest controllers.

Chiroptera: The scientific order that includes all bats. It's characterized by its members' ability to fly, making them the only mammals naturally capable of true and sustained flight.

Conservation Status: A classification given to species based on their risk of extinction. The International Union for Conservation of Nature (IUCN) Red List categorizes species from least concern to critically endangered, providing a measure of the urgency of conservation efforts needed.

Ecosystem Services: The benefits that humans obtain from ecosystems, including natural processes and materials. Bats provide ecosystem services such as pest control, which benefits agriculture by reducing the need for pesticides, and pollination, which supports the reproduction of many plants.

Endangered Species: Species that are in danger of extinction within the foreseeable future throughout all or a significant portion of their range. Conservation efforts aim to protect these species from threats and restore their populations.

Foraging: The act of searching for food. Bats forage for various foods depending on their species, including insects, fruit, nectar, and, in some cases, small vertebrates or blood.

Guano: The excrement of seabirds and bats, used as fertilizer. Bat guano is particularly valued for its high nutrient content, but it also plays a role in ecosystems, supporting cave environments and providing nutrients for other organisms.

Habitat Fragmentation: The process by which large, continuous habitats are divided into smaller, isolated sections, often due to human activities. This can have detrimental effects on wildlife, including bats, by isolating populations and reducing access to food and roost sites.

Insecticide Resistance: The ability of insects to withstand the effects of insecticides through genetic mutations. Bats help manage pest populations naturally, reducing the reliance on chemical pesticides and the risk of developing resistant pest species.

Migration: The seasonal movement of animals from one region to another. Some bat species migrate to take advantage of seasonal food supplies or to find suitable climates for hibernation or maternity roosts.

Pesticide Impact: The effect that chemicals used to kill pests have on non-target wildlife, including bats. Pesticides can reduce the availability of food for insectivorous bats and poison bats directly if they consume contaminated prey.

White-Nose Syndrome (WNS): A fungal disease that affects hibernating bats, named for the white fungus that appears on the muzzle and other parts of infected bats. WNS has caused significant declines in bat populations in North America.

Wildlife Corridor: A strip of natural habitat connecting populations of wildlife that have been separated by human activities such as roads and development. Wildlife corridors can facilitate movement and genetic exchange between isolated bat populations.

These definitions offer a glimpse into the complex and fascinating world of bats and the efforts to conserve them. Understanding these terms is crucial for effective communication and education in the field of bat conservation.

Appendix

Creating a bat house requires precise planning and design to ensure it meets the needs of the bats you aim to attract. While a comprehensive guide with diagrams is beyond the text-based nature of this platform, I can provide a detailed description to guide you through designing and building a basic yet effective bat house. For visual plans and more intricate designs, it's recommended to consult resources from reputable conservation organizations like Bat Conservation International or similar entities.

Here's a detailed outline to get you started:

Materials Needed:

- 1 sheet of 1/2" exterior-grade plywood or cedar board (for durability and resistance to weather)

- 1 piece of 1"x2" (3/4" x 1 1/2" finished) wood strip for the roosting chamber divider

- Exterior-grade screws

- Non-toxic, water-based paint or stain (darker shades for cooler climates, lighter for warmer ones)

- Caulk to seal joints

- Sandpaper to roughen interior surfaces

Tools Required:

- Saw (hand saw or power saw)

- Drill with screwdriver bits and drill bits

- Measuring tape

- Level

- Paintbrush

- Caulking gun

Construction Steps:

1. Cut the Plywood: Based on your design, cut the plywood into pieces for the back, sides, top, bottom, and front panels. A typical bat house can be about 24 inches tall, 16 inches wide, and 3 to 5 inches deep, divided into two chambers by a central piece of wood.

2. Prepare the Interior: Before assembling, roughen the inside surface of the back panel and the divider to help bats grip the surface. This can be done by cutting horizontal grooves every 1/2 inch with a saw or attaching non-toxic, rough mesh fabric.

3. Assemble the Bat House: Attach the sides to the back panel using screws, ensuring the top and bottom are open. Then, insert the divider to create two chambers, securing it with screws. Attach the bottom piece, leaving a 1/2-inch vent gap above it for air circulation.

4. Attach the Front Panels: If your design includes a landing area (a protruding bottom part where bats can land and climb up), attach it now. Then, attach the front panels, leaving a 3/4-inch slot open between them as the entrance.

5. Seal and Paint: Caulk all exterior joints to ensure the bat house is weatherproof. Once the caulk is dry, paint or stain the exterior to protect it from the elements and help regulate the interior temperature.

6. Install the Bat House: Choose a sunny location, ideally facing south or southeast, where the bat house will receive at least 6 hours of direct sunlight daily. Mount it on a pole, building, or other structures, at least 12 to 20 feet above ground. Ensure it's securely attached and stable.

Placement Tips:

- Avoid placing the bat house too close to bright lights.

- Ensure there is a clear flight path to the entrance.

- Place near a water source if possible.

Maintenance:

- Check the bat house at least once a year for wear and make necessary repairs.

- Look for signs of occupancy, such as bat guano beneath the house.

- Clean out any wasp nests during the off-season when bats are not present.

For detailed diagrams and additional design options, such as multi-chambered bat houses that can accommodate larger colonies, it's beneficial to consult specific bat house construction guides from wildlife conservation organizations. These resources often include plans tested and optimized for success in attracting bats, along with tips for monitoring and maintenance.

Contact Information for Bat Conservation Organizations

For detailed guidance, support, and resources on bat conservation, contacting reputable organizations dedicated to the protection and study of bats can be immensely helpful.

Here's a list of prominent bat conservation organizations along with their contact information:

Bat Conservation International (BCI)

-Website: [Bat Conservation International](http://www.batcon.org)

- Email: info@batcon.org

- Phone: +1 (512) 327-9721

- Address: 500 N Capital of TX Hwy., Building 1, Austin, TX 78746, USA

BCI is a global leader in conserving the world's bats and their habitats through conservation, education, and research efforts. They offer a wealth of resources on bat conservation, including guidelines for building bat houses, protecting habitats, and educational materials.

The Bat Conservation Trust (BCT)

- Website: [Bat Conservation Trust](http://www.bats.org.uk)

- Email: enquiries@bats.org.uk

- Phone: +44 (0)20 7820 7168

- Address: Quadrant House, 250 Kennington Lane, London SE11 5RD, UK

BCT is dedicated to the conservation of bats and the landscapes on which they rely. They provide information on bat conservation in the UK, including how to get involved in local bat groups, advice for living with bats, and bat conservation research.

Organization for Bat Conservation (OBC)

Please note that as of my last update, the Organization for Bat Conservation has closed. However, its legacy continues through other organizations and resources available online. For alternative sources of information and support, consider the above organizations or similar entities dedicated to bat conservation.

Bat Conservation Africa

- Website: Information may be available through broader conservation organizations or research institutions focused on African wildlife.

Bat Conservation Africa works towards the conservation of Africa's bats and their habitats. Given the diversity and number of bat species in Africa, efforts are often region-specific, focusing on research, habitat protection, and community engagement.

Australasian Bat Society

- Website: [Australasian Bat Society](http://ausbats.org.au)

- Email: Use the contact form on their website.

- Address: Provided upon request through their contact form.

Focused on the conservation of bats in Australia and the Australasian region, this society promotes the conservation and study of bats by providing information on bat rescue, research, and how to get involved in conservation efforts.

North American Bat Conservation Alliance (NABCA)

- Website and Contact Information: NABCA collaborates through various organizations in North America, including Bat Conservation International. Refer to BCI for resources and how to get involved in North America.

NABCA works to promote the conservation of bats in North America through collaboration between organizations, government agencies, and individuals.

Merlin Tuttle's Bat Conservation

- Website: [Merlin Tuttle's Bat Conservation](https://www.merlintuttle.org)

- Email: info@merlintuttle.org

- Phone and Address: Available upon request through their website.

Founded by renowned bat expert Merlin Tuttle, this organization focuses on bat conservation through research, education, and public outreach, emphasizing the positive impacts of bats on ecosystems.

When reaching out to these organizations, be specific about your interests or needs, whether it's about starting a bat colony, bat house installation, or participating in conservation efforts. These organizations can provide expert guidance, resources, and opportunities to support bat conservation.

www.ingramcontent.com/pod-product-compliance
Lightning Source LLC
Chambersburg PA
CBHW061645250726
48659CB00004B/1378